It occurred to me

An irreverent and humorous yet
serious retrospective on Public Service

by

Sir Peter D Carr CBE

Grosvenor House
Publishing Limited

All rights reserved
Copyright © Sir Peter D Carr CBE, 2016

The right of Sir Peter D Carr CBE to be identified as the author of this
work has been asserted in accordance with Section 78
of the Copyright, Designs and Patents Act 1988

The book cover picture is copyright to Sir Peter D Carr CBE

This book is published by
Grosvenor House Publishing Ltd
28-30 High Street, Guildford, Surrey, GU1 3EL.
www.grosvenorhousepublishing.co.uk

This book is sold subject to the conditions that it shall not, by way of
trade or otherwise, be lent, resold, hired out or otherwise circulated
without the author's or publisher's prior consent in any form of binding or
cover other than that in which it is published and
without a similar condition including this condition being imposed
on the subsequent purchaser.

A CIP record for this book
is available from the British Library

ISBN 978-1-78623-899-3

To Geraldine for being there

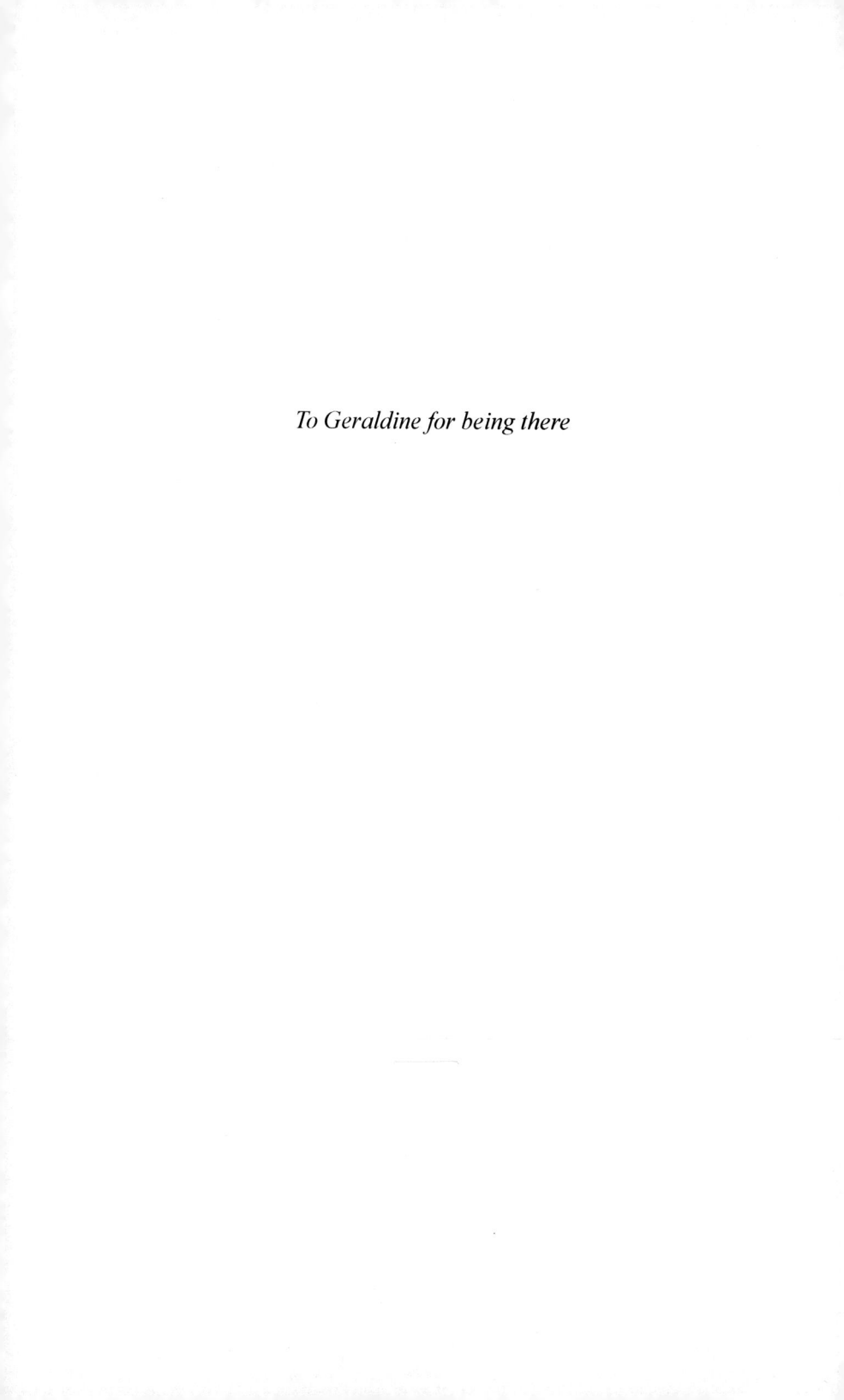

Foreword vii

One **Silver Spoons** 1
a dirty old town; printing and politics; town roots; maturity at thirteen; impressions; shaking loose; stepping out; minimalist military

Two **The Breakout** 17
Finland & beyond; college on a shoestring; a Ruskin story; moving again; schools for adults; from Hull, Hell and Halifax; shop stewards; the Oxford School; Derek Robinson; Paris and Stockholm

Three **Donovan and After** 40
The CIR ; the right return; the ConMech saga

Four **Civil Service 64** 52
the miners' strike; visiting America; the London-bound commuter ; a conciliatory time

Five **Diplomatic Credentials** 62
Washington DC; George Meany ; the AFL-CIO and the TUC; the Labour Attaché's role; immigrant labour ; Republicans return; labour law in two countries; leaders great and small; brazil nuts; Washington and wider ; diplomatic immunity; ambassadors three

| Six | **Home Again** | **110** |

… to trouble…; an art lesson; leading the City Action Team

| Seven | **The Firing Line** | **123** |

a move to the National Health Service; a contractual quirk; getting my own back; the deprivation factor ; taking advantage; secretaries of state; pensions and other things; returning to the NHS; bringing about change; the '7 No's';

Postscript	**150**
Bibliography	**154**
Index	**156**

Foreword to the Second Edition

In this second edition of my memoirs I have included substantial material on people, places and events that I feel should be explored more than I chose to do in the original edition. For example, the 2015 movie *Selma* revived memories of meetings and discussions with five leaders of the Civil Rights movement portrayed in the film. Then again, after visiting Ruskin College in Oxford it was apparent that the great educational contribution made by that institution was now in the past and this required acknowledgement and comment. My friendship and involvement with Derek Robinson and his dramatic role in the Pay Board decision in the 1973 Miners' strike needed to be more fully explored, and the role of the Labour Attachés, both British and American respectfully reviewed. Finally, the National Health Service occupied me for 26 years after I retired and that experience demanded description and room for strong comment. It was a great privilege to serve the NHS over such a long period and in such influential positions. These took me through very different political regimes and a range of political solutions to meet the eternal challenge of the NHS, the polarized positions of quality and budget control.

The title of this biographical piece sets out its theme – it is about events and ideas. A few family members and colleagues, having read the draft, commented that I deal only in brief with personal relationships. Where I do so it is in the context of an event or a particular circumstance in which I found myself. Most of my close family appear only briefly in the text but this is not a measure of their influence; on the contrary the emotional impact of our relationships shaped me and set my direction.

All those named in the text are absolved from any responsibility for the views and the ideas expressed here. I have endeavoured to avoid self-aggrandizement and there are many pages of humorous self-deprecation. Having worked with many, I am severe in my criticism of only one politician. Events are described from my distinctive perspective and I acknowledge that there will be different interpretations. I set out the part I believe I played in the harmony of events. In other words, it is my cadenza.

I owe a debt of gratitude to Professor David Mervin for reading through the text and suggesting valuable alterations, and my grateful thanks to Anne Dart for her tireless contribution in typing out the draft but also in correcting and improving the whole document.

A couple of sentences in a Foreword is no way to set out the contribution to one's life of a marriage to a remarkable lady. It justifies a book beyond my capacity. Suffice here to record my eternal love and gratitude to Geraldine.

In its composition this labour has had our grandchildren in mind so they might know a little of their grandfather and his times. To Nelson, Warren, Elizabeth and Oscar, I dedicate this text.

One Silver Spoons

It was a hot and humid October in 1978 when we arrived in Washington. I had a diplomatic visa in my passport and diplomatic credentials filed with the State Department. I had a new job ahead and the stimulating prospect of studying that immense country from within. At the Embassy my in-tray was spilling over with paper and on top a note, from a distinguished ex-union and Labor Department official, invited my wife and me to dinner that weekend. Over the meal they asked me how I had got there. I said by plane to which they laughed. "Now," they insisted, "you must tell us how *you* really got *here*." So I told them.

A dirty old town

My sharpest early memories are of war: 1939 and an August holiday in Blackpool with the sultry evenings outdoors excited by the fencing searchlights limbering for a conflict to come. Then sitting with my father sometime later perched on an athletic field wall giving welcome and other comforts to Dunkirk veterans. Or huddled under a bed in a hospital isolation ward, fevered with diphtheria, head protected with an enamel basin, cringing at the occasional wham of an explosion and window glass splintering into the room. I recall being pretty upset too on leaving hospital to find my friends in possession of fine collections of shrapnel, which they displayed on their bedroom shelves.

My father's allotment fed us well throughout the war. He skillfully preserved new potatoes in sand, saving many for our

Christmas dinner. He was also good at developing contraptions to make life easier. His device in response to the blackout lowered a tube over the room light when the outside door opened.

My mother's ingenuity ran to organizing the steady supply of nourishing food from the butcher and the grocery stores. Even in the midst of the worst shortage she could always produce food. She was skilled at managing our tiny budget and never failed to ensure the availability of funds to provide our annual holiday. For her it was an essential and treasured glimpse of other places, which she determinedly ensured we experienced all through the war years. My father, bless him, could not save, but my mother stashed away the necessary pennies throughout the year to ensure our annual joy. She continued with considerable ingenuity, over the austerity years following the war, to find ways to accumulate the required funds. A brilliant whist player with a photographic memory, she could play a skillful hand with the sole intention of adding to the 'holiday pot'. Some years later, with a regular supply of waste materials from a local clothing factory, she produced thousands of dolls and draught excluders in the shape of dachshund dogs – a very popular item in a town with open fires and badly fitting doors. A few years later she drove my father to the point of distraction when she purchased a knitting machine. It is no exaggeration to say that she virtually clothed the whole town in a range of woollen sweaters and cardigans. To any hint of criticism of her dedication she would simply retort that holidays needed to be longer and should be spent in decent hotels.

In his younger days my father was an accomplished sportsman – a soccer player with sufficient talent to be invited to join Sheffield Wednesday junior team and with the drive, co-ordination and pace to make him a valued bowler sought after by local cricket teams. As a young man my father nurtured an ambition to achieve professional status in both sports, and might possibly have achieved his ambition without the ultimatum from my mother. She posed the necessary economic question. In an age when athletes were admired but unrewarded, my father was forced to choose between the glamour of sport and the harsher reality of married life. From there he contented himself with weekend sport and a more secure, but certainly duller and more routine economic existence.

Printing and Politics

Those early war years hold other formative memories. My father was a printer and managed the rotary machine shop of a weekly newspaper. I loved my regular visits to his workplace. Hot metal newsprint production has a smell redolent of last minute exclusive news headlines; of caustic editorial wit; of honest reporting borne of hard labour. I was always captivated by the linotype machine, which was an almost perfect conception in its original design and was hardly altered throughout its productive life. It worked with a satisfying series of mechanical clunks and on many of my visits would produce my name and address as a special treat.

The men who worked these hot metal machines were as distinct in character as the machines on which they laboured. They were literate labourers! They read more than the material they produced: they had ideas, studied books, attended libraries and talked intelligent politics over their beers.

Of all early memories, the Friday nights from this period provided inspiration and energy for many years. Friday saw the final edition of the newspaper put to bed. With luck and no mishaps in the earlier stages, the vast rotary machine would complete the production around 11 pm. My mother worked throughout the evening in sequence with the printing. By 10.30 pm, with the table laid and possibly a large rabbit pie in the shiny black Yorkshire stove, she would be ready to welcome my father, and frequently his colleagues. With the house so perfumed by the cooking it would have been a rare torture to dispatch a child to bed despite the hour. As the eldest son I often joined the adults for the meal and frequently caught the tone of the ensuing debate.

Those years, from the latter stages of the war into the depressing years of austerity that followed, were materially mean and constricting. But down the years I carry no sense of a people beaten down by a lack of material well-being. On the contrary, I have a clear memory of debate, of ideas, of propositions for political reform; of a belief in democratic politics and of the value that working people would bring to that process through their active participation. That perception is reinforced by the memory of those rabbit pie dinners and the optimism with which my parents and their friends engaged the political and economic troubles which faced them. From those dinners I recall not only optimism but also an enthusiasm for the political process, which in the ensuing years has been squandered in the arrogance and incompetence of our parochial parliamentary system. Maybe my parents and their friends were to some extent looking for solutions to problems that could not simply be resolved within the parliamentary system. Maybe they were all as much part of the problem as they were the agents of the solution. Ernest Bevin, in a telling speech in the United States, once said: "The problem with my people is the poverty of their desire." While unbridled avarice and greed can rip a country apart, lack of individual aspiration can, as Bevin saw it, flatten off the broader economic wellbeing and development of the general population.

When we look around our older industrial cities and their inheritance of mean housing, in which generations continue to be born and grow, can we doubt the wisdom of Bevin's dictum? When I return to my home town and look at that depressing terrace which contains my birthplace at No.1 Briton Street, still occupied by a young family, I think of the optimism of those Friday night debates.

Town Roots

My mother's family can be traced back through the history of the town as far as written records extend. Her mother owned a bakery and provisions store, which is still remembered by a dwindling number for the quality of its brown cobs and crusty loaves. I recently talked to an old gentleman who showed me his first pair of cuff links, bought from Woolworth's seventy years before. On purchasing them he had proudly rushed round to show to my grandmother in her shop. He described her as the 'economic heart' of the family: hardworking of course, but with the added contribution of shrewdness and skill. Harriet came to live with us in her later years, but I remember her only as a frail and lonely old lady.

My grandfather Harry Tailby's existence within our family history somewhat resembles those retouched photographs of Stalin's purged friends, where those he had eliminated were painted out of existence. I could never persuade my mother, her sister Gertrude and certainly not my grandmother to talk at any length about my grandfather. I know that he had worked as a senior manager in a manufacturing company and I have heard him described by those who knew him as a 'Gaffer's Man'. He certainly seems to have been skilled in the art of language. He belonged to an expensive golf club, knew everybody in town and had an enviable skill with the ladies. For a time he worked successfully as an auctioneer, but over the years he seems to have drained my grandmother's business of any profit in order to finance his golfing and other activities. He was a close confidant of a notorious character by the name of Jack Harry White, who was an undertaker by profession. On occasion, just for the hell of it, my grandfather would volunteer to drive a horse-drawn hearse. When I was a young man, Jack Harry told me of more than one occasion when my grandfather galloped the hearse through the town high street at break-neck speed.

Grandfather eventually flew the family nest to set up a new life with a younger woman. Maybe the failure of the bakery under his consistent plundering precipitated his departure, or maybe the attractions of the younger woman were too strong to resist. Poor man, he had little time for his new life before he suffered a stroke and lay bedridden in hospital. Yet I still award him some admiration. When my grandmother visited him in sympathy for his plight, she found that his original girlfriend had left, but that he had so charmed a visitor to the adjacent bed that she had agreed to take him into her home. He died shortly after that, but his persuasive skills, his style, and his love of life, somewhat too great for his modest income, are still remembered with affection. Who knows but that some of his more admirable traits have passed down the generations to manifest themselves in the present!

Maturity at Thirteen

I left full-time schooling a few days before my 14th birthday. No one could later explain how I managed that feat, but some minor illness provided the excuse and the war that was still raging in 1944 certainly contributed. To my young unsophisticated mind, all the future opportunities were there to be grasped outside the school system. I saw the Grammar School as an alien institution filled with students from owner-occupied houses. The Technical School seemed to me unattractively full of teachers who looked for all the world like machine shop foremen.

On reflection I wonder at the stupidity of my determination to throw myself into the deep end of industrial life – and a very deep end it turned out to be. I entered the joiner's shop in the GEC factory in Swinton and life there provided the first steps in craftsmanship, together with a few other hesitant lessons in life. My mentor in the joiner's shop was a fine craftsman of the old school who guided me through the first stages, in which I acquired some elementary skill. At an early date I was taken through the traditional task of building a toolbox for myself. The protocol demanded lessons in constructing dovetail joints and in finishing the wood down to the required width. I still possess the toolbox some 70 years later, though I honestly cannot say that I look at it with any pride. I had other tasks pressed upon me in my early days in 'the workshop'. I made a mallet and constructed the body of a wooden smoothing plane. When I now wander around antique shows and see, listed as antiques, tools of the kind I constructed as an apprentice, I feel my age.

The GEC factory was sloppily managed, with little formal discipline imposed. I soon learned that the whole factory could be explored at will and without challenge, every department stopped at and every attractive girl visited, so long as I carried a few sheets of official-looking paper. The woodworking shop had many periods of low pressure, so my forays into the excitement of the production lines were fairly frequent and I developed a familiar relationship with people, especially the ladies, in each of the production departments.

By the end of 1944 the allied victory against Germany had lowered the physical tension of war in this country but it had released an intense emotional urge to celebrate. Christmas 1944 in that factory provided the excuse for a celebration, which turned the production lines into a wild drunken feast. With my 'official' bits of paper I set off to explore this behaviour first hand. In the end I had to run for my life in front of various possies of females who yelled all kinds of promises of action they would take should they catch me. I ran fast in those days.

By early 1945 the War Department had already cut back on its orders for new aircraft. The war with Japan came to its violent conclusion as the experiments at Los Alamos were extended to Hiroshima and Nagasaki. The Swinton factory shed its labour and I faced my first redundancy before I had reached the age of 15.

The Woodworkers' Union ran a fairly effective information service, so within three or four days I continued my apprenticeship with a cabinet maker /funeral director and jobbing builder. The workshop had few mechanical aids apart from a planing machine and a circular saw. In consequence all the hardwood for the furniture or the coffins had to be cut and finished by hand – a long and tedious task. Yet it was an exercise, which in its repetition encouraged the development of skills that stood me in good stead during the years ahead.

About this time I began to read again. I enrolled in an evening class at my old school to study English Literature, and under some loose guidance began both to read and to write. My friends and work colleagues regarded this exercise as distinctly odd! I should, in their view, have been engaged in technical studies. Despite my tutor's efforts my reading tended to be governed by caprice and prejudice and I flashed from one point on the literary spectrum to the other. Of course I absorbed the standard left-wing texts – *The*

Ragged Trousered Philanthropist; every text of George Bernard Shaw's work I could obtain, various novels by Maxim Gorki and a few works by H.G. Wells. But I also found an appreciation for Rudyard Kipling and was so captivated by one gifted book of short stories by Damon Runyon, *Blue Plate Special,* that I recall reading it three times through without a break. There were many other volumes, some rejected when the language and concepts assumed more than I could bring to the interpretation. But I managed to struggle through some Wordsworth poems and a few novels by D.H. Lawrence.

Impressions

It was around this period that a visual image had an impact upon me. It was so indelibly marked my consciousness that I can still recall my emotional response to this day. The image of the Holocaust I saw on the flickering screen of a *Pathe* Pictorial Newsreel at the Majestic Cinema so disturbed was my 15 year-old stomach that I had to retreat to the toilet. I do not remember if I managed to sit through the main film, but I do know that the black and white images of the bodies dressed in stripes, piled high with the topmost still slightly moving, have remained in my mind's eye ever since.

That impact of the brutality of man was later replicated in another context. I read John Hersey's book *Hiroshima* soon after its publication. In his book he records the horror of the atomic bomb explosion on that city in 1945. Until reading that book I admit that in my preconception the Japanese were not high on my list of nations to be preserved. When the two atomic bombs were detonated over the Japanese cities I responded, as any young nationalist would do, with loud cheers. In Hersey's book I had to deal with the brutality of a bomb which killed and mutilated thousands of civilized and sophisticated men, women and children and continued its destruction of lives over the following generations.

As men and women from the forces returned home from the war the newly-elected Labour government, both representing and being charged with the increasing aspirations of the voters, set about the immense task of post-war reconstruction. The building industry formed a central plank in the government's regeneration programme and it soon became apparent that it was going to provide some useful job opportunities. From my youthful and inexperienced viewpoint the industry seemed to offer a variety of work and companionship, with fresh air as a bonus. Naturally I had not reckoned with the ferocious winters to come.

I joined a scheme that had been organized to train apprentices in the skills of the construction industry. Around thirty teenage apprentices worked on the scheme under adult supervision and were charged with the task of completing the construction of twenty houses. We drove the supervisors to distraction with our games, but eventually completed the task. The houses are still standing and, I presume, still house twenty families.

Shaking loose

In the 1970s, unemployment brought economic ruin to most of the industrial working class communities in Britain. Coal mining communities were particularly badly affected. Not that these were areas of affluence in the 1940s and 1950s. Although coal miners headed up the manual worker income scale in the 1950s their traditional lifestyle provided little in the way of luxury. In the post-war period the town of my birth had little culture, no music beyond the annual performance of Handel's *Messiah*, no theatre but for an occasional visiting repertory company, no art, and its architecture was uniformly dull. But, thanks to Mr. Carnegie, it had a sparsely stocked though well used library, in which I spent considerable time.

In South Wales the mining villages were vital communities. Miners' welfare centres housed lively activity and debate. Many of the South Wales collieries had leisure centres with well stocked libraries which fed the intellectual and political appetites of the miners. Oddly, when in the 1920s depression the South Wales miners tramped north to the still working Yorkshire coalfields, they brought with them little of that Welsh nurtured appetite for knowledge, music and debate.

In the 1940s and '50s my home town was a dead urban centre, stifling in its conformity. Social pressure flattened the aspirations of the bright, and mocked any deviation from the acceptable mundane. The downward social pressure protected the sensitivities of the majority, who subconsciously recognized that in all probability they were sentenced by fate, or sod's law, to spend the rest of their lives in the boredom of that depressing place. It was not easy to break out, but some notable characters had done so: a founder of the Canadian Social Credit Party, a leading Grand Prix racing driver, a subsequently wealthy television writer. But the act of leaving required purpose, effective process, money and determination. This last vital quality I had inherited in abundance from my mother, together with her full encouragement for my purpose. Throughout her life she longed to leave that place, but sadly, (apart from some gloriously enjoyable holidays) she never managed to do so.

I had inherited a restless nature from my mother and I constantly played with schemes to change occupation, or move town, or even to emigrate. With strong support from my mother, I pursued the prospect of emigration to within a hair's breadth of moving to Canada. In the end I stayed with my familiar life, in the expectation that I could soon be on my way to a parliamentary seat.

Stepping out

Reaching the age of maturity at 21 meant more than the achievement of a skilled qualification; it led in the 1950s to a two-year detachment to the military as a National Service recruit. It was a prospect that held no attractions, despite my ambition to be on the move.

Before I took on the mould-breaking experience of military service I travelled with a friend to Belgium, making my first journey abroad. We went by boat from Immingham to Ghent, staying with a generous café proprietor in that city who had been friends of the family before the war. We spent an interesting week there before accompanying our hosts on their vacation, camping in the village of Echternach in Luxembourg.

For Belgium, a country divided by religion and language, this was a particularly disturbing period and we found ourselves on vacation in the centre of a revolution. The Café Louise owned by our hosts was located in the old dock area of Ghent but had plenty of residential and some retirement homes around it. The café next door employed a pretty girl who worked as a prostitute, with whom we spent many hours in earnest conversation; though neither my friend nor I had enough of a grasp of the Flemish language to take the conversation very far.

Opposite the café a multi-coloured stone wall ran half the length of the street. We were shown, one evening, some peculiar chips and indentations in clusters along the wall. I had made some juvenile comment about the German occupation and in response some of the café clientele took us outside to show the bullet marks sculptured in the wall through its use by a firing squad in the early years of the occupation. One café client had seen his brother shot; another had seen his best friend killed there. I was amazed that they still came to the Café Louise to sit, talk and drink their Stella beers as though it were simply a recreational place beyond the reach of the tensions and problems of their daily lives.

After a week we departed from the Café Louise and headed for Luxembourg in Frank's Citroen, piled high with camping equipment. The low-slung black Citroen induced in the two immature British minds the vision of the Gestapo, so we played the game from the backseats of the car all the way to Echternach, much to the consternation of our generous hosts.

It was an idyllic holiday and the weather, as always in memory, is now remembered as hot and conducive to outdoor adventure. We talked to anyone who looked to be in any way responsive. We traded on our curiosity value – the British were not a travelling nation in those days- and we made many friends. After chatting to an attractive girl cycling from the shops we were repeatedly invited

Silver spoons

to visit the family of a Count on the edge of town. The family obviously delighted in English conversation. However we grew tired of the exercise once we recognized that our effort was taking us no nearer to the attractive granddaughter.

Many years later I took my whole family, Geraldine, Steven and Alyce, on a camping holiday in Echternach. One evening, Geraldine, following my eye roving over the attractive occupant of a neighbouring tent, observed that she could well be the daughter of the beauty I pursued on my previous visit. How dispiriting!

On that first youthful visit, just before we packed the tent for our return to Ghent, the campsite seemed to generate an unusual level of agitated discussion among the campers. A plane passing over the campsite, followed by two military planes, caused some sharp discussion and friction among people on the site.

It turned out that King Leopold had declared his intention to return to Belgium and claim the Belgian throne. The quality of his relations with the German military during the occupation had been widely interpreted by many in Belgium as collaboration, and a wide body of opinion opposed his return. The natural fracture in Belgian society between the Walloons and the Flemish began to widen.

On our return we set off on our journey from Luxembourg to Ghent, planning to stop for a meal in Brussels. News on a radio before we left told of a march to Brussels initiated by a modest hundred or so opponents of Leopold. We had problems entering the capital city and circled around the outskirts, finally entering alongside a stream of marchers estimated at 500,000 strong. As we entered the city searching for a quiet place to eat we realized that Brussels was already occupied by King Leopold's opponents. I have a memory of a cortege of flowers on its way to the Palace, donated by an order of nuns, being overturned in the square in which we had settled for our lunch. We made a rapid departure.

At last we arrived in Ghent to discover the docks immobilized by a general strike and with our journey home to England in jeopardy. King Leopold finally abdicated in 1951 in favour of his rather unambitious but diplomatically skillful son, following a national referendum on the monarchy. To his great credit King Baudouin made a crucial contribution to the unity of his fractious nation over the 42 years of his eventual reign. As I write this text the daily newspapers are reporting his death and from all political sides they report the wide respect of his people.

Minimalist military

July 1951 I completed my apprenticeship as a carpenter and joiner and then received instructions to report for military duty to RAF Padgate for basic training, or 'square bashing' as it is more accurately described. It proved to be the usual mindless process of confinement to camp for seven weeks of parade ground drill, during which the non-commissioned officers yelled at us in an impossible attempt to reshape our determinedly free spirits to fit the needs of the military.

On the second weekend, the boredom of another Saturday afternoon and Sunday confined to camp was persuasive enough to see me through a gap in the fence and past the outside guardroom to spend a welcome weekend at home. I thereby began my military service as I was to continue it for the following two years, escaping at every available opportunity.

Following Padgate, a complement of 36 recruits, all time-served and skilled woodworkers, were dispatched to St. Athan airbase. An unfortunate corporal, with little more than ten weeks' training in the skills of woodcraft, was detailed to instruct us in the basic elements of the craft. To his credit he quickly responded to the challenge and, abandoning the original programme, he channeled our talents into the construction of a yacht for the RAF St. Athan sailing club. That task occupied virtually all the 16-week training period, following which we were posted to our service stations.

A longstanding friend and I had attended the military pre-service assessment and medical tests together. He chose to nominate the Mountain Rescue Service as his preferred service option: I chose Air Sea Rescue. We should have reckoned with the perversity of the military mind, which saw me posted to Inverness and eventual attachment to the Mountain Rescue Team and his posting to the Southampton Air Sea Rescue Unit.

The Dalcross Camp, now Inverness airport, to which I was posted, had been closed since the end of the war and then reopened in response to the Korean conflict. We found it to be fairly primitive, though the small British Airways lounge offered some civilized relief once we won the favour of the friendly staff. On a few occasions I persuaded the crew of the BA Rapide biplanes to take me on their round trips to the islands. The plane schedules were frequently governed by the tides, landing as they did on the beach.

At Dalcross I joined with a colleague, by the name of Major Platt, to form the Dalcross Music Society and with a generous grant of funds from the education officer we set out to purchase a range of recordings to suit our taste. I cannot recall any other participants for the many winter evenings we spent with the music. For my part I fed on Major's extensive musical knowledge.

Apart from the musical evenings, the treks into the mountains with the Kinloss Mountain Rescue Team, and independent weekends exploring the magnificent scenery, my main occupation seems to have been the exploration of schemes for legitimately detaching myself from the camp. I developed a friendship with a pilot who by chance had a girlfriend in Doncaster. Many weekends we flew to the town, returning early on Monday morning.

I then found the provisions of the educational service to be of assistance and enjoyed two separate 14-day detachments to Nottingham University. It was during this time that I realized my need to return to full-time education.

Having taken two programmes at the university, that educational avenue of escape from camp routine was blocked by some regulation, so some other means would have to be discovered. I sought freedom through physical adventure; but I should have known better. Volunteering for parachute training, I found, may bring release from daily routine, but it substitutes a ritual which threatens death if it is ignored. I jumped, or to be strictly accurate

I was thrust, from the plane by a corporal. I did not take kindly to the experience.

Jumping provided another military experience and from a far less dramatic height it almost saw the end of me. One weekend, with no prospect of a free flight to Doncaster, I purchased an unwanted travel warrant from a colleague. The journey by train from Inverness to Edinburgh entailed few problems apart from the tediously slow pace. At Edinburgh, late in the day, I boarded a London-bound train only to find, as we left Darlington, that the train had no scheduled stop before London. The train passed through York at high speed and promised an equally rapid track through Doncaster. I was foolishly desperate, having no money and too little time left in the weekend to travel to and from London. As the train whipped through Doncaster station, its brakes were applied to slow down, in deference to a well-remembered train crash on a bend by the bridges beyond the station. The braking and total darkness led me into a false sense of the actual speed and, after gaining the complicity of a fellow passenger to close the door behind me, I launched myself from the train into a black void. As I let go I realized the stupidity of my action, I floated through the air and hit the ground very hard. I came round with a railway lamp in my eyes and a railway worker shaking me into sensibility. He pulled my limp legs from the track across which I had fallen with urgent shouts to move before a train came roaring along that very line. My uniform persuaded the railway worker to allow me to limp away without reporting the event to his superiors. Following that foolish event I spent the best part of a week in hospital with an injured foot. On return to the camp, despite my best endeavours my plastered leg and other bruising gained no sympathy. "Injured alighting from a train lad", questioned the duty officer. "And how fast would that train have been going at the time?" I spent a week confined to punishment duties but my injuries and limp ensured that the duties were fairly light. My two-year National Service typically came to a close during an absence from the camp. One evening I began to suffer increasing pain in the gut. At some time after midnight I staggered to the guardroom and demanded attention.

Being laid out in Inverness hospital recovering from an appendectomy was not how I had planned to celebrate my demobilisation. It was anything but keyhole surgery, and on my return home my father felt it appropriate to arrange for me to stay for a couple of weeks with an old colleague, Harry Dark and his wife in Jersey. Harry had worked on the island throughout the war and German occupation and had many stories to tell of some of his and his friends' subversive activities. He impressed upon me the need to make firm plans for my future. He urged me to go back to school. He warned that if I failed to be decisive then events would conspire to subvert my ambition. When I returned from Jersey I knew where I intended to go. Before I could make that future a reality I would need to go back to hard labour in the construction industry in order to raise the money I needed for college.

Two THE BREAKOUT

Finland and beyond

In the summer of 1956 I made a journey to Finland to join the summer camp of the International Union of Socialist Youth. The journey to Tampere took us by train through Germany and Denmark across the ferry to Gothenberg. From Stockholm the overnight journey to Finland had a magical air. We lay in sleeping bags on deck with the late June sun sitting on the horizon lighting all the archipelago islands into various shades of pink. At the camp in Tampere the long daylight hours raised a problem. After hours of sport, debate, singing and social intercourse the sun would finally dip below the trees across the lake, but within the hour the light would change its quality as the sun began its ascent and the damned birds began their dawn chorus. Tents, I discovered, are far from sound-proof.

Though the camp participants were drawn from Europe and Scandinavia, we discovered some friendly fellows with American accents. They were dressed casually but somewhat unsuitably for camping. American government policy, at that time, strongly favoured a greater political unity in Europe and the democratic socialist movements in the various Western European nations were in line with that desire. They were also for the most part strongly anti-Communist, and this too found favour in Washington.

The British contingent on the camp, as always, arrived with no uniformed shirts, no shorts, and no football boots or other sporting gear. We needed to face up with style to the challenge of the Germans in a sporting competition. I prevailed on our American colleagues, who admitted that they were there to foster good relations, to fund the purchase of football gear for the British team. The cash came in a roll of notes: the only condition being my agreement to sign a US Government headed financial receipt! We lost the game, but as always we were sporting losers.

At the finale of the Finnish camp the programme promised a grand march of all the national delegations to take place before invited dignitaries from the host city, culminating in a grand concert on the shore of the lake at sundown. The German delegation, mainly from the Falcon movement, were dressed in smart uniforms, which to our prejudiced British eyes looked too much like the recently discarded outfits of the Hitler Youth. They also sported a range of colourful pennants on poles, which gave them the appearance of a well-drilled and efficiently oorganized group. By contrast the British were dressed in motley and rather shabby attire, and a Union Jack for a parade would have been the last thing any of us would have thought to bring to Finland. We thought to make one but on the edge of abandoning the idea I decided to call on the British Consul in Tampere. He was a charming fellow, married as I recall to a Finnish lady, and was delighted to loan a flag or two to such patriotic chaps! I asked him what had happened to the Consulate Office during the war, conscious of the fact that following the Soviet attack on that tiny country Finland had allied itself with Germany during the rest of the war. The Consul looked surprised by the question, saying that nothing had happened and that he had stayed on as Consul throughout. When I asked about the flag flying outside his consular home, he proudly maintained that it had flown throughout the War. I never did check out that story with the Foreign Office, but prefer in any case to believe it is true.

On my train journey back from Finland I occupied the hours with Steinbeck's *Grapes of Wrath* and determined that, like the 'Okies', I would pack my bags and depart from my previous lifestyle.

College on a shoestring

In 1956 Fircroft College was still run with that sense of idealism which had inspired George Cadbury to establish the institution. He did so after one of his visits to Denmark had allowed him to see a Danish Folk High School at work. The Principal, an intellectual and saintly fellow called Leslie Stephens, ran the college with a total conviction that the adult students would be socially and intellectually transformed by their one year's experience. I wrote to him on my return from Finland to ask if I could apply, at that late stage, for a place in the coming academic year. I was accepted and applied to the county authority for a grant towards the fees. The interview panel at the county had a blunt Yorkshire businessman in the chair and a jolly Labour Councillor who unfortunately fuelled my exasperation at the stupidity of the questions and comments. The final questions and display of ignorance from the panel encouraged me, foolishly, to issue a sharp rebuke. "Do you read lad?" asked the chairman. "Yes sir"' I replied. "And what are you reading now?" he asked. I told him that I had just completed Steinbeck's *Grapes of Wrath*. "Is he an American?"'he asked. The whole line of questioning had already indicated a total lack of sympathy with my ambition. So I replied that it was not for me to advise them of such a fact when they were the ones charged to judge me. I kept the letter from the county for many years. It said that the majority of the committee had judged me to be "not yet mature enough to warrant a grant." I was then 26 years of age.

Nevertheless, Leslie Stephens urged that I should not be deterred and he managed to find a small amount of money to cover the fees. It was with great joy and anticipation that I boarded the train for Birmingham and from there by bus to Bournville. The College enrolled only 36 adult students, with around a third of them from the Commonwealth, so we enjoyed the luxury of nearly one-to-one guidance throughout our studies. That year the college moved into George Cadbury's fine house, bequeathed to it in his will, and I left my own mark there, returning to build fittings and furnishings in vacations over the next year.

It was in Bournville that I met Geraldine, felt a compelling attraction and rashly asked her to marry me. I have never for a moment doubted the wisdom of that decision but I can only speak for my part of that enduring union. We met 'romantically' in a gas showroom doorway on a blind date organized by a friend. A year later I sent a card to Geraldine with the following bad verse inside:

> *Love, a most discerning bard*
> *once said, Will walk where wise*
> *men fear to tread, But never told us*
> *how we're drawn*
>
> *Into that foolish state forlorn*
> *Oh! that I had some such warning On a*
> *certain rainy morning Bachelorhood—thy*
> *noble freedom's tomb Sealed in the door of*
> *a gas showroom*
>
> *So let me warn you, dodgers*
> *of the cherubs dart 'Tis not just*
> *cupid who can spear the heart*
>
> *Since one short year ago, I lay infirm*
> *A victim to that heater—Mr. Therm!*

Following Fircroft I moved my studies to Ruskin College Oxford. In some ways that move signified a temporary lack of confidence. I should have gone with the opportunity and taken an available place at the University of Keele. But Ruskin had been in mind over the years and it seemed to offer a more 'classical' education for an aspiring candidate of the Left than a provincial university. Mistake or not it proved to be a formative and stimulating two years and a period in which we established some enduring friendships.

Among the most enduring of these friendships I count Professor Jay Blumler as one of the strongest. Jay's lectures in politics at

Ruskin at that time gave coherence to my unstructured thoughts about politics. The clarity of his thinking and exposition of political theory lasted with me through the years. Jay went on to establish a School of Public Communications at Leeds University and developed a worldwide reputation as one of the great thinkers on political communication. He retired from Leeds, but continued to contribute to his international reputation and in fact won a lifetime achievement award after retirement from the American Political Science Association. He and I saw each other throughout the whole of our working lives and he continued to contribute to my thinking well into both our retirements.

Lunch time in Oxford gave me the enjoyable opportunity to walk around the city – a short stroll that always provided a new interest. One June midday, while passing near the Mitre pub on the High, a rather matronly lady grabbed my arm and begged for assistance. She offered me £10 for an 'easy task' that could be accomplished in half an hour. The intriguing nature of the request should have advised caution, but the £10 offer to an impoverished married student overwhelmed the more cautious instincts. Mrs. Duffy said that the task would simply be to accompany her to her home on the Iffley Road and stand next to her as she gave notice to quit to a tenant of the downstairs room. At the first sign of my cautious acceptance she thrust me into a nearby taxi, which sped us to the Iffley Road. However, as the taxi pulled up in front of the house I caught a first glimpse of the tenant and a premonition of trouble to come. Running from the house there appeared a very angry young lady, one hand on hip and the other clenched into a waving fist. As we climbed out of the taxi the young woman launched herself on Mrs. Duffy with a clear intention of doing her some considerable harm. I stepped between them to keep them apart and with the pushing and pulling of their attempt to do battle I managed to choreograph the three of us into the doorway of the large Victorian terrace. I thought that the mutual belligerence would reduce when we were no longer providing entertainment for the neighbours, but I clearly had that wrong. The volume and the physical nature of the argument seemed to increase. From the yelling I detected that Mrs. Duffy had cleared the young lady's belongings from the room and refused to declare where she had taken them. For her part Mrs. Duffy wanted the young woman out of the house that day. But there were other strands to their argument that indicated many more complex issues. Partly out of self-preservation I eased the girl into her room, but needed to close the door to keep out the householder, who was still venting her anger by means of a loud percussion on the door.

I then turned to the girl, who asked what I was doing there, so I told her, at which she gave out a grim laugh. "Do you know what this is about?" she asked. I shrugged. It transpired that Mrs. Duffy, a doctor's widow, had let three rooms to three young ladies working at the world's oldest profession. Applying for planning permission for a property development next door, Mrs. Duffy had been strongly advised to get rid of the ladies to remove the cause of any possible objections. "But I have called the police," the girl said. "The old witch stole my belongings and threatened me with violence."

At that point I finally realized the highly compromising position into which I had manoeuvred myself. Here I stood in an Oxford brothel, locked in a room with an attractive young woman and with the police on their way. All of this I would need to explain to my heavily pregnant wife. A young policeman tapped on the door. He had no interest in explanations but just wanted my address. He then suggested that I leave with some speed, which I attempted to do, but I was now accosted by an irate taxi driver who insisted that I pay him and threatened to call on the support of the young police officer. As I walked back to the College I remembered Mrs. Duffy's £10 payment which, of course, I had failed to collect.

That afternoon I spent some time constructing the way I would explain to Geraldine the extra-ordinary series of events, my honourable intentions and the sheer innocence of my presence there in Iffley Road.

I think she believed me!

For the two years in Oxford we rented a caravan in the grounds of the Bickfords' house in Forest Hill. While I grafted away on essays and in pushing back the frontiers of my knowledge my new wife worked to keep us. Again our grant was too small, deliberately not recognizing my married status.

Our personal financial crisis came to a head during the stress of the final examinations. In a perfectly timed bit of family planning Geraldine lay in the Churchill Hospital in the final stages of labour. Between visits I tried to mug up some of the detail for the exam papers I was facing each day in the Examination Schools. In the midst of this drama the Calor gas ran out, we had literally no food in the larder and the last few shillings from my final student cheque had drained away. This was real trouble and I refused to turn again to my parents following their past generosity. In desperation I wrote to the Woodworkers' Union General Secretary to describe my plight. It must have been a convincing letter. By return post he sent a £50 cheque, which allowed us to survive until my mother skillfully organized our rescue from Oxford.

That gesture by the Woodworkers' Union might seem little, but it was so immediate and unconditional that I determined to pay back their generosity. Though no longer involved in the craft of the industry I continued my membership of the union until their grant had been returned with interest. Indeed many years later, the redoubtable Clive Jenkins publicly described me as the only member of a TUC affiliated union ever to have served in the Diplomatic Service. It is a record which must surely have been surpassed with the affiliation into the TUC of the First Division Association, the top level civil servants' union.

So much for the drama and hardship. But what of my academic studies? I took the opportunity to sit, always captivated, through as many lectures by A J P Taylor as I could fit into the timetable, attended a number of sessions by Isaiah Berlin and participated in the formative seminars conducted at Nuffield by Alan Flanders and Hugh Clegg.

The Breakout | 23

It was at one of these seminars that I brazenly set out to take apart the thesis presented by a very young but clearly intellectually challenging Peter Jay. Luckily he had forgotten the face, if not the event, when it came to my interview with Ambassador Jay in the Foreign Office prior to my Washington appointment. In the industrial relations part of my studies I faced some tough opposition from my tutor for challenging the then orthodox Ruskin view of collective bargaining as a political expression of working-class solidarity. My politically incorrect essays, influenced by the works of John Dunlop, were returned with as much comment written into them by my tutor as they had in original text by me.

Having completed the Diploma in Politics and Economics (Dip. Pol. Econ., Oxon) I should have stayed in Oxford to continue for the degree, and Balliol College seemed sympathetic to that ambition. However the struggle to persuade the authorities to provide another grant seemed hopeless. With a son as well as a wife our financial plight was desperate, so a teaching course with secure funding seemed the best option. I continued to regret that choice for some years.

A Ruskin story

A fair number of Ruskin students went on to change the course of history in one field or another, either significantly or modestly, within their own spheres. In one particular case a period of study at Ruskin had a profound effect. Tom Mboya had established and led the Kenya Local Government Union, which was the country's largest official trade union and political movement. Mboya went to Ruskin on a grant from a British Labour Party scholarship fund and spent just one academic year, from 1955 to 1956. His contemporaries at the College claim that he relished every day of the year and that he emerged with increased confidence and the assurance of a leader.

In the 1950s Kenya, still under British rule, was in economic and political turmoil. An insurgency, mainly involving the Kikuyu tribe, began around 1951, to which the British responded with almost unrestrained force. The British authorities identified the Kikuyu as the tribal generators of the disruption and prohibited any Kikuyu political activity, disbanded any organizations they led, and arrested their leaders. The head of the Kenyan Africa Union, Jomo Kenyatta, and five of his close colleagues were arrested, tried and sentenced to seven years imprisonment, along with five hundred others.

Being of the Luo people, who were largely unengaged in the activity, Tom Mboya had a degree of immunity from the turbulence. He became Kenya's prominent political figure, leading protests against the trials and the British repression. By the time Mboya came to Ruskin the Mau Mau activity and the reactionary British repression was easing, but Kenyatta remained imprisoned until 1959. Mboya continued to petition for Kenyatta's release while at Oxford and continued that campaign on his return to Kenya. Once back from Oxford he formed the People's Convention Party and gained election to the Kenyan Legislative Council. With Kenyatta's eventual release and the achievement of independence under a Kenyatta government, Tom Mboya had a significant role to play in ministerial office as a representative of the minority Luo people.

Mboya acknowledged the significant role that the year at Ruskin had played in his development. He sought to find the funds to extend the provision to a wide range of Kenyan and East African actual and aspirant political leaders. Britain was largely in withdrawal mode in Africa and not looking to fund education programmes in the way Mboya proposed. Undeterred, Mboya turned to his influential contacts in the States, where the campaign for the Presidential election probably played to his advantage. His organization sought the support of Vice President Richard Nixon, who turned the request down. Mboya's team then made contact with George Meany, the AFL-CIO President, whose response was sympathetic and helpful. The union approached the Democratic Party organization, where Sargent Shriver, John F. Kennedy's brother-in-law, picked up the request and saw immediate advantage for Senator Kennedy's campaign. Shriver chaired the well-resourced Kennedy Family Foundation, which promised to support the project.

In my discussion with Meany many years later he told me of his high regard for Tom Mboya and his distress at the news of Mboya's murder in 1969. With Meany, Mboya's proposal to establish a foundation to enable East African leaders to undertake a period of university education fell on fertile ground. It fitted well with his growing conviction that the AFL-CIO should be directly engaged in international activity. Meany lent his strong support in the approach to his favorite politician, Senator John F. Kennedy.

In 1959 Mboya had enough funds to pay the air fares and other travel costs for 81 Kenyan students, who went to various American universities that year. He spoke at a mass rally in Washington the same year as Martin Luther King and Bayard Ruskin, and gained the backing of Harry Belafonte. Then in 1960 the Kennedy brothers, John F. and Robert, fulfilled their promise of support, providing a $100,000 grant from their family trust. Having initially rejected the project, the State Department sluggishly came in to offer longer-term support. The African/American Student Foundation was then firmly established. Among the 81 students that first year was a member of the Luo ethnic group enrolled at the University of Hawaii: Barack Hussain Obama, father of President Obama.

It is interesting to contemplate that, were it not for the valued year Mboya spent at Ruskin, then the United States might never have had the benefit of its first black President. Acknowledging this debt, President Obama has referred to Tom Mboya as his 'godfather'.

Moving again

Following our rescue from Oxford we spent another year surviving, this time in London, where I qualified to teach. The course itself was straightforward enough, but the economic struggle to complete it lent real drama to the year. The college at the Elephant and Castle was housed in an old workhouse – a fact that my wife and I found to be entirely appropriate in our financial circumstances. We ate the basic necessities, walked everywhere, pushing Steve for miles in the family donated pram, and our ill-fitting clothes were cast offs from the family, except for Steve, who was dressed like a prince by his grandparents.

To save on bus fares I frequently walked all the way to college from the Forest Hill area of South London where we lived. I took to eating lunch in a white tile café which seemed to cater for the homeless. I found that I could dine on two scoops of potatoes for two pence and have the luxury of parsley sauce for an extra penny. None of this seemed to be too bad at the time, for we knew it would not last. I had determined that in good time I would be sitting in the House of Commons, complete with striped trousers, maroon tie and matching socks and be charged by my constituents to take forward the radical changes needed both to increase our national wealth and to ensure its equitable distribution!

In all seriousness, I had in fact thought through where I would wish to make a political contribution, and that would be in housing policy. It seemed to me then that both major political parties brought stereotype phrases rather than policy into their approach to housing. There continues to be a strong element of truth in that view, and no government in those intervening years has brought with it any comprehensive strategy which integrates housing into its other economic and social policies.

Schools for Adults

An effective educational system both reflects and changes the society it serves, and the balance between the two is crucial. Originally Fircroft and Ruskin served a radical social purpose in a society that has now undergone an enormous transformation since the two Colleges were founded. The pace of change continues to accelerate, and demands an increasing proportion of the population should have the intellectual capability to organize within rapidly adapting systems, and engage with and exploit the expanding capability of new technology. In its response to these demands higher education has more than doubled in size since I arrived at Fircroft. Age is no longer a barrier to university education, as I am pleased to note when I attend the Academic Congregations at universities and observe the wide age range of those receiving degrees.

In the 1950's I belonged to a class of ill-equipped, under-educated, deprived but socially engaged and ambitious young people, rejected by an elitist and generally inflexible education system. Higher and further education has now adapted to meet changing demands, and consequently Fircroft and Ruskin no longer exist in their original form. The only constant is their names. Nevertheless, without hanging on to the archaic I have some regrets about the way the changes were carried out in the two Colleges. In the case of Ruskin its conversion seems to have been accompanied by the destruction of a major part of its historical records. The process of burning the past in order to establish the future is not generally associated with Oxford. The role Ruskin played since its establishment in 1899 by two postgraduate students, Walter Vrooman and Charles Beard, is in the DNA of the families of ex-Ruskin students worldwide. As Vrooman pointed out, the College would have a central role in transforming society. Ruskin he said, would take men and women "who have merely been condemning our institutions and would teach them instead on how to reform them." From that date it had a profound impact on the lives of young men and women who had struggled to find a way into full-time higher education. It was a comprehensive education system and it catered both for the intellectually brilliant and the less bright, but profoundly altered all of their lives.

Fircroft was established ten years after Ruskin and its founder, George Cadbury, had a different perspective on society from Beard and Vrooman. Cadbury's liberal Quaker traditions conditioned him to be greatly attracted to the objectives, practices and philosophy of the Danish Folk High Schools. These were, and for the most part still are, non-formal residential adult education institutions taking young people aged 18-24 for programmes of study lasting around 4 months. They all study along the lines of their particular interest and do so in an environment which the Danish Government has proudly described as having an "emphasis on general mind-broadening education."

There are 70 Folk High Schools in Denmark. The majority concentrate on teaching young students during the winter, but open up to all ages for the summer short course season. Over 50,000 Danes attend the Folk High Schools each year, which remarkably amounts to 2% of the total population.

My regret is that Fircroft has not stayed within its original liberal tradition promoted by George Cadbury and that it failed to reject the utilitarian approach that led to its transition into its present vocational form. Denmark's society and its democratic institutions are greatly strengthened by the Folk High School movement. Its population is more deeply engaged in the the arts, literature, philosophy and music as a result of this long educational tradition.

From Hull, Hell and Halifax …

After the London year I had to find a job in teaching. I owed the banks a large amount of money, loaned to see us through the four 'indulgent' college years. The solution to the linked needs of job and house seemed to be a teaching job in a town so short of teaching talent that a house would be provided as a recruiting inducement. For good or ill that decision led to a teaching post at the Further Education College in Halifax, which came with a pretty depressing flat on a windswept hill on the outskirts of town. We had no furniture, not even a bed to furnish the flat. My mother organized a furniture removal van, provided a deposit for a couch which doubled as a bed, and she instructed the removal men to clear out for us all the furniture from the whole ground floor of her house. God only knows what my father said when he returned from work to find the place completely bare. My mother simply waved us off with the cheery view that she had tried all ways to get new furniture and generosity was simply her ultimate sanction in her bid for something new.

The Halifax job proved to be hard graft with little compensation. I formed a Fabian Group in town and we enjoyed a few evenings with Edward Thompson, who was then busy writing his classic *Making of the English Working Classes*. In the run-up to the general election of 1964 I organized town meetings, factory gate meetings and visits to social clubs for the Labour Candidate Shirley Summerskill. The general election results were predictably close, and Halifax gained considerable publicity with the contest between Maurice Macmillan, son of the former Prime Minister, and Shirley Summerskill, the daughter of a well-known Labour Minister. Shirley emerged as a charming and intelligent candidate, but unnervingly unsure of herself when she had to meet with her potential supporters. I steered her around various events, guiding her towards people she should meet, persuading her to shake hands with people and promoting opportunities for her to speak. At the same time Geraldine organized a series of coffee mornings hosted by ourselves or other active women and to these we invited only women we knew not to be actively engaged in politics.

I also organized a major eve of the poll conference at which MP George Brown was billed as the major speaker. He arrived late and hoarse from his hundreds of previous speaking engagements. Striding to the platform to loud applause, some of it in sheer relief at his eventual arrival, he yanked at the microphone to adjust it but instead pulled it from its socket. As he stared at the two pieces he exclaimed: "Good God, I've made a mess of this!" His words broadcast across the hall. A bright young fellow in the front took the opportunity to yell the comment that it signified the mess Brown would make if he and his colleagues were returned to office. Brown then deftly slotted the microphone head back into its socket and responded that when he and his colleagues messed things up, they had the skill and good sense to know how to put matters right. I suspect that he had practiced that trick at every stop in his campaign—never failing to draw out the waiting victim.

Our daughter Alyce was born in Halifax. It was a joyful occasion for all of us, including young Steven, who took such pride in the event that one might have assumed he had achieved the creation of a sister single-handed. He was never jealous of the intrusion and wanted always to care for his sister. Alyce was born in the middle of the worst winter for years and we found the severity of the climate compounded by our elevated position, perched as we were high on a Pennine hill. As Geraldine began her labour pains I ran to a neighbour's phone to call an ambulance but with the road too treacherous for the vehicle to complete the last 200 yards up the hill she had to walk down to meet it.

Following her return home with Alyce the great freeze softened a little and a recently installed heater on the top floor thawed out the main water pipe from its frozen and fractured state. We were deluged with a cascade of water, which effectively destroyed three apartments and their belongings, thankfully missing us by a whisker.

Shop Stewards

At the college in Halifax I began one of the first day-release courses for shop stewards to be run in the country. To put the programme in place I had to persuade the local engineering employers of its value and to engage the unions in the promotion of the course. It was no easy task, but I was assisted by an agreement between the then British Employers' Confederation and the TUC, which called for the widespread development of shop steward training. Beyond the far left rhetoric of class conflict and the arguments for industrial strife to improve working class power, it was painfully obvious that British industrial relations were bedeviled by a sheer lack of comprehension between the parties. They were literally schools apart and culturally disparate. If a conflict of interest is inevitable between those at work and their employers, then at least it should be a conflict conducted with clarity of understanding.

Some years later I visited the Employers' Confederation in Sweden, where they told me of a walk-out by the door-keepers in the building. The employer organization offered the venue for the mediation of national disputes. As the employer or trade union officials arrived they needed to be steered to the confines of their separate rooms, but convention had never allowed the posting of notices. The doorkeepers had the task of judging into which group each arrival fitted. Finally the doorkeepers had walked out in protest against their impossible task. The parties looked alike, wore equally good suits, could not be distinguished by their accents, and not even the newspapers they carried could be used to distinguish them. I recognize that it was a judgment in the context of a very different social system, but the search for solutions to Britain's chronic labour relations difficulties offered opportunity for various solutions, and the Swedish system seemed then to be attractive. In truth Swedish collective bargaining was not all sweetness and light. Some tough decisions had to be faced; but it seemed that their disputes were centred on matters of substance, less on major misunderstanding, and rarely derived from a sheer lack of trust arising from class incomprehension.

Our shop steward courses were not aimed at achieving industrial tranquility, but at the effective working of agreed procedures. However it soon became apparent that disruptive misunderstanding arose from the fact that the agreed system was as much unwritten as it was written. The teaching material came from various sources. Apart from my own materials I received some interesting papers from Fred Hoehler, then teaching autoworkers in Michigan. He provided a number of ideas that I adapted for our own programmes. In Oxford Arthur Marsh had developed a series of teaching documents linked to the procedures pertaining to engineering industry disputes. He generously allowed me to go through his filing cabinets and, where two documents existed, I was permitted to take one.

The Oxford school

For all this experimental work with unions and matching work with supervisors, I found Halifax to be a constricting and insular environment. A change of environment was needed to expand the work and, rather sadly, I concluded that the new environment would be in the South, where it was possible to find a more liberal approach by the colleges and a greater response by the local employer associations. So, in the summer of 1964, we moved south to Essex. The move coincided with a growing national concern for the disruptive nature of our collective bargaining system. The reconstituted employer organization (the CBI) and the TUC were persuaded by the Labour government to work out the basis on which they would agree a policy to influence the movement of prices and incomes. Following an agreement on the basic principles they went on to decide the appropriate machinery for implementing that policy. By this jointly agreed approach the National Board for Prices and Incomes (NBPI) was established with the support and participation of all the major parties involved in collective bargaining. It was a process in which I was determined to play a part.

Major Oxford academics were recruited into various roles in the NBPI. Both Alan Flanders and Hugh Clegg had begun to establish the case for the reform of collective bargaining and the basis on which they believed those reforms should be promoted. Flanders had established his thesis in his widely influential analysis of the Esso Fawley Productivity Agreement. In his view British industrial relations were bedeviled by two systems of collective bargaining, one existing in the mass of written and mainly archaic jointly agreed procedures, and the other system within the informal conventions and practices which governed the effective behaviour, particularly at plant and workshop levels. I recall Flanders illustrating his thesis with the example of a building industry shop steward whose role and function were unrecognized in any of the written negotiating procedures or any of the formally agreed rules. Yet the building industry stewards existed in reality and were at that time powerful figures in the determination of effective pay at site level. It was no good, said Flanders, defining unconstitutional action as being unacceptable in those circumstances. How, he asked, could the building stewards abide by procedures which denied their very existence? In Flanders' view we needed to develop procedures which met the needs of the parties and reflected their effective relationships. They needed to be jointly agreed procedures and the two sides then required to abide by the agreement.

The second strand of the Oxford thesis applied to payment systems, and Derek Robinson was a leading thinker in this field. Many industries had developed a complexity in their pay systems which defied effective rational control. Many pay systems were only tenuously linked to achievement in some industries. For example in Fleet Street, locus of the London newspaper industry[1]

---

1 The National Newspapers were at that time housed in and around Fleet Street.

The Breakout | 33

at that time, the dynamics of the pay system owed more to the interplay of shop-floor power politics than to productivity, profit, or the effective contribution of the workforce.

Soon after my appointment to the Essex College I was pleased to be drawn into the NBPI's work as one of its Industrial Relations Advisers. In that capacity I worked on a number of the major questions referred to the Board by the Secretary of State. I conducted case studies in the engineering industry, on collective bargaining procedures in the building and construction industries and on various aspects of productivity bargaining, which the Board sought to promote as a central part of its activity. I also worked on various general references and themes examined by the Board.

The NBPI in its early days looked to many as though it might succeed where other instruments of government had failed. With the retrospective gift of hindsight its inevitable failure is all too apparent. On the credit side the Board's research illustrated the wide-ranging problems with pay systems. Its reports continued to be influential for many years after the Board's demise and many thinking employers, consultants and academics involved in the reform of management and pay systems continued to draw on the evidence and distilled wisdom in the Reports. However, as a central instrument in a voluntary incomes policy the Board stood no chance of achieving long-term success. When it came to effective control the Board found its functions swept aside by the 1966 sterling crisis, which led the government to abandon voluntarism and to legislate against pay and price increases.

One has to say, again in hindsight, that certain central assumptions underpinning the Board's functions had more than a little arrogance and elitism running through them. In broad terms the assumption that a small band of highly intelligent academics employed to illustrate the truth of pay systems can, by that process, effectively control them against the pressures of the labour market and the combined ingenuity of unions and employers now looks both naive and hopeless. The real impact on pay came with the devaluation of sterling in 1967. With all the many economic problems facing the country it was an electoral wonder that Harold Wilson managed to convert his slender majority into a solid working majority in the 1966 election.

Derek Robinson

Derek and I came from neighbouring mining towns in Yorkshire. As he himself put it: "We originated from the same coal seam." His father worked as a coal miner in Derek's home town of Barnsley. His background honed his temperament, fired his convictions, and endowed him with his accent. His significant contribution on Public Boards is well recorded. He exerted international influence through his work with the International Labour Office; with the National Board for Prices and Incomes he helped shape the nature of the debate. Together with Barbara Castle, the Employment Secretary, he engaged in the design of a national policy. At the Pay Board, in dramatic circumstances, an intensive media spotlight fell on him in the midst of an election campaign and tested out the true calibre of the man. He came through with distinction. During the whole time, of course, he kept up his commitments as a distinguished Fellow of Magdalen College Oxford, a college he loved.

We had bumped into each other at Ruskin College, which he continued to frequent, but our first real *encounter* came in what became regular Saturday morning visits to the launderette in Headington. I use the word encounter because that is what it was. I haven't a clue what subject engaged us, but recognized that I had met a remarkable intelligence. Each Saturday had a different subject, on which he would demonstrate his mastery of detail, an instinct for the nuances of a debate, and a lightening way of trapping his opponent in any ambiguity. In my last talk to him only a few weeks before his death he fondly recalled those debates.

Paris and Stockholm

During my period with the NPBI I earned my principal income from the college in Essex, where I headed the branch which promoted a whole series of part-time, residential and block release courses in labour relations. With my colleague George Healy I went to see Jack Jones, the Transport and General Workers' Union (T&GWU) General Secretary, and obtained his agreement to take all the dockworker shop stewards through a basic training course. At the time of our meeting with him Jack had been in office only a few days, but with the bronze bust of Ernest Bevin looking over his shoulder he looked and behaved as though he had been there for a decade. He agreed to our proposition for the training programme, but saw to it that we began our intake of stewards with the whole of the No.1 Docks Group, which had the reputation of being the toughest and most battle-hardened dock stewards in the business. We survived the experience and the programme ran its full course.

By the late 60s, however, the docks were on the verge of massive changes. The casual basis of employment had been replaced with a basic wage under a general contract with the Dock Labour Board. But before the new employment security had time to settle in, the industry began to experience radical changes in technology. The conventional method of shipping loose cargoes began to disappear and containerized cargoes were introduced, backed in some cases by roll on and off methods of transportation. It was only a matter of time before the old labour practices were eliminated by the technological and system changes.

The work in Essex brought us into fairly close working relationships with most of the trade union leaders of the time. Vic Feather, first as Assistant then as General Secretary to the Trades Union Congress (TUC), was a strong supporter and a regular contributor. Clive Jenkins appeared on a number of occasions and Alan Fisher, General Secretary of the National Union of Public Employers (NUPE), gave many sessions linked into our programmes. We also sought to introduce occasional controversy from outside the union ranks. Enoch Powell, the right-wing Tory MP, attended and outlined a thesis to prove that, in the longer term, unions have no effect on the real level of earnings. A fair number of employers also made regular contributions. These broader educational sessions were peripheral to the central objectives of most courses, which were primarily aimed at improving the knowledge and bargaining techniques of the participants.

At one point we proposed to open the programmes to an occasional overseas experience. Already the docks stewards had visited Rotterdam to see the effects of fully containerized and computerized cargoes. To widen this overseas experience I wrote to a number of union federations overseas to see if any wished to establish reciprocal visits on mutually agreed training programmes. The Swedish Labour Organization proved keen and we had exchanges that ran for some years. Early in 1968 I had a letter from the French CGT Union Federation which proposed that their education officials visit the College to hold discussions on a possible exchange. The letter caused a few problems, the CGT having its established traditional political base in the French Communist Party. The TUC said, "Go ahead but don't formally tell us." I was keen for a number of reasons: for a start the CGT seemed to be an effective union force in France: it had a strong membership in the automobile industry and its perspective on events promised to be challenging.

In return for the CGT's exploratory visit I was invited to Paris to see their facilities and to pursue the difficult issue of the programme for the exchange. It was May 1968, with Paris in the grip of the student revolt. My hosts were CGT officials and I had no doubts as to their political affiliations. They met me at Beauvais airport, and on the journey into Paris they corrected one major misconception on my part by fiercely denouncing the student revolt as the work of middle class *gauchistes*.

Paris, in that May and June, was a divided city, both geographically and across the age barriers. In one part of the city the cafés remained full and the conversations seemed as they always were. Cross a few streets and the tension was extreme. Everywhere the garbage mounted and public transport was virtually non-existent. At my foolish request the CGT officials took me to the Sorbonne, where in a nearby square students stood in groups in each case with an older figure in their midst. The tutors were apparently seeking to cool tempers and pacify the students.

Suddenly from our vantage point in a café we saw that the square had been ringed by helmeted riot police clustered into vans. The police moved out of the vans, formed ranks, pulled down visors and moved into the square from all sides. My host yelled and we sprinted for our car a few yards away as the police swept through the square like a double blue wave, one rank behind the other. One fierce fellow began to beat the roof of our car with his baton and at the behest of my host I pressed my passport to the window, yelled "Tourist!" and waved us through. As we left the square I turned to witness the students undergoing some pretty rough treatment. Within a few hours some 20,000 students were on the streets, digging up cobbles and fighting a pitched battle with the police.

By coincidence my principal host for the visit had an undergraduate son at the Sorbonne who was active in the revolt. The father strongly denounced his son's activities, but to pacify the curiosity of a visiting Englishman he arranged through the son's contacts for us to meet with some of the student leaders. I was sorry to miss the opportunity to meet Daniel Cohn Bendit but I did get to talk to Alain Geismar and Jacques Sauvageot. During another trip across town I was taken on a surprise visit to the Folies Bergere theatre, where all the performers were on strike and occupying the theatre. I made the awful comment to a group of the ladies that theirs was the only strike which entailed putting on clothes.

We also called in to see the clandestine publicity centre organized by the students to support their campaign. At that time the main French television stations had a practice of rating programmes judged unsuitable for children by indicating a little box in the left corner of the screen. Among the many remarkably striking posters hanging up to dry, like washing on a line, one poster had a pointed impact. It had no words, just a cartoon of General de Gaulle with a small box in his mouth.

A few weeks after my visit to Paris the Gaullist Party were returned to office winning a massive victory in the French elections, and the whole student revolt seemed a lost cause. In fact, against the wishes of his Prime Minister, the President set about the introduction of significant and wide-ranging reforms of the French higher educational system that few of the students I met during my visit would have believed possible under that Presidency.

Three Donovan and After

The Commission on Industrial Relations (CIR)

The year of my visit to Paris also saw the publication of the Royal Commission's report on *Trade Unions and Employers' Associations*, commonly called the Donovan Report. The Commission had worked on its study for three years and its research reports, published at intervals, had provided useful teaching material. Alan Flanders' evidence to the Commission, in which he propounded his theory of the two systems of collective bargaining, the formal and the informal, became the central thesis of the Donovan report itself. From that base the Commission rejected propositions for the introduction of various legal provisions and sanctions to limit and contain strikes. Instead it called for a substantial reform of the system through voluntary agreements.

The Commission went on to recommend the registration of all major collective agreements and for a permanent Commission with access to the agreements and with the responsibility to negotiate reforms. The Donovan recommendations were accepted by the Labour government but in addition the government attempted to give itself some reserve legal powers to be held by the Secretary of State.

The Commission on Industrial Relations (CIR), established the year after the Donovan publication, had George Woodcock, recently retired General Secretary of the TUC, as its chairman and Alan Flanders as one of its board members. The Commission took on the task of promoting radical changes in collective bargaining structures by subjecting a single company or an entire industry to a thorough and detailed study and from that to establishing general principles. The Commission also had responsibility for determining union recognition cases, but without the legal authority to enforce its recognition decisions.

Soon after the CIR had been established I had a call from the Secretary to the Commission, Norman Singleton, to ask if I would be willing to see him in his office, and if convenient that very afternoon. I burdened my teaching colleagues with my classes and with excitement caught the train to London.

I remember some searching but typically polite questions from Norman, who concluded with two questions: "Do you want to join us?", and "When can you start?" The Commission expected to be buried under references from the Secretary of State, Barbara Castle, and its staff needed to be in place to take charge of them. I went back to college, negotiated my release with the help of a generous principal and three days later I joined the CIR. My second day at the Commission proved to be a day of some considerable external excitement. From my office I looked out on a massive trade union demonstration winding its way along Kingsway in opposition to the Labour government's proposition to provide for itself the reserve legal powers which it had proposed in its cutely entitled White Paper, *In Place of Strife*.

The deluge of references from the Secretary of State never materialised. The spirit of voluntarism extolled by Donovan had translated into the principle that any reference to the CIR should be first approved by both the TUC and the Confederation of British Industry (CBI). For a long period both sides effectively prevaricated on all cases. The high expectations built around the CIR's birth began to ebb away as it lay dormant for almost four months.

When the references finally came through, we employed many of the skills developed in previous work with the NBPI. An inquiry into a company required a thorough and systematic analysis of the informal and formal bargaining arrangements, the details and the actual dynamics of the payments systems, the power structures and responsibilities in management and workforce, together with a clear understanding of the production and technology in the company.

My first task took me into a chemical company, Associated Octel, to head an inquiry into the plant where a union recognition demand had challenged management's historical belief that supervisors were part of management and management did not join unions. The company was not obstructive to our inquiry but they did not regard the Commission as objective. We were not in the business of pushing people into collective bargaining, but we nonetheless drew our general assumptions from Donovan – that collective bargaining was the best means of regulating the terms of employment. With that assumption and in the context of its time, it was highly unlikely that the Commission would find against a workgroup claiming collective bargaining rights.

The International Harvester inquiry offered another kind of challenge. The two factories in Doncaster and one in Bradford had suffered a constant and high level of conflict. I led a talented team sent in by the Commission and we virtually lived in the factories for seven months, putting both systems and behaviour through a rigorous analysis. Finally we recommended substantial changes to the pay system, designed a new procedure and negotiated it into agreement with all parties. The whole process, strongly supported by the local MP Harold Walker[2], was one of the Commission's most successful cases. Of all the CIR's work, the Harvester case probably came nearest to proving the central contention of the Donovan Commission and demonstrating the potential of CIR procedures.

In that early period of the CIR we enjoyed a good working relationship with the top union leadership. As the references came

---

[2] Appointed Minister of State at the Employment Department, then Deputy Speaker and went finally to the Lords

through we had the need to meet most of the union leaders, and they generally supported our activity. On two references we had the interesting experience of dealing with Reg Birch, a national official of the Engineering Union. Reg was a total romantic in his politics and a perfect gentleman in his personal behaviour. He would assiduously walk around the table to shake hands with everyone at the commencement of a meeting and insist on repeating the procedure at the conclusion, regardless of the numbers involved. In the meeting he brought a sharp experience to bear on issues and a skilful defence of his members' interests.

Along with most of his fellow communists Reg felt politically disoriented by the impact of Russian *glasnost* on the world communist movement. He centred his attention on China, and founded the 1968 offshoot Communist Party of Great Britain (Marxist-Leninist), also serving as its first Chairman. At one of our meetings he offered sincere apologies for his inability to attend a follow-up meeting, with the explanation that he had a visit to China planned for that time. As we left the meeting room I quipped that he should give my very best regards to Mao Zedong. He politely called me back and solemnly explained that he understood Mao to be seriously ill, and that on this occasion he would be unable to convey my regards. I subsequently learned that Reg did indeed have access to the very highest level of the Chinese hierarchy.

It was around this time that Reg became involved in an event at the Ford Motor Company that is now established in the anecdotal history of collective bargaining. With colleagues he attended a meeting at the company to hear of proposed changes to the employment conditions. The union representatives were submitted to a long and stiflingly boring presentation on pension benefits, during which a repeated knocking occurred, presumably from the door. An inspection by a junior manager ascertained that no one stood outside. The presentation started again and once more the knocking began. After another repeat performance a manager saw Reg with his fist below the table and asked if he had a point to make. "No,"' said Reg. "It's not me. But it is my members who

Donovan and After | 43

have passed away since this boring session began, wanting to know if these benefits are retrospective."

I once asked Reg what he did at weekends. He said that he looked through all his newspapers and newssheets to discover what demonstrations were planned. Then he would spend a long time in debate with family and friends deciding which side to support. He was a determined, committed and wonderfully humorous man.

The right return

The General Election of 1970 brought a Conservative government to power with a commitment to introduce a body of labour law as the basis for a wide-ranging reform of industrial relations. Under Geoffrey Howe's guidance, the Act of 1971 brought in a complex of interrelated legal provisions which owed much to United States labor law. Within the 1971 Act the CIR continued its broad reforming role and retained much of its voluntarist approach. It continued to retain its assumptions about the efficacy of collective bargaining, but it was charged to receive its recognition cases from the newly established Industrial Relations Court, under its senior judge Sir John (later Lord) Donaldson. George Woodcock resigned from the Commission with other union official board members. Many of the staff with union backgrounds quickly found other jobs.

I had arranged with George Woodcock for him to speak to a major conference in Thurrock organized by my colleague George Healy. The arrangements had been made well before the unforeseen election, so I found myself travelling with Woodcock to Essex. The occasion was set against the background of the newly proposed 1971 legislation, already spelled out by the government in outline, together with the proposal to engage the CIR in the legal process.

George was a taciturn man at the best of times, but that evening he was as gloomy as the night outside the car. He told me of his earlier conviction that the Commission could have radically changed our industrial relations practices but that public patience had run out. It was no good just blaming the press: the unions would have to shoulder the blame for their failure to convince the broader public of their legitimacy. They would need a sympathetic ear inside the system and they would unofficially use it.

I had known George Woodcock for some years. He was a regular visitor to Ruskin during my time there and had interviewed me for a job at the TUC which, thankfully, he had determined was not for me. Woodcock had a powerful intellect, which enabled him to grasp the wider implications of events. That night he was a deeply saddened man and from the platform, as he concluded his speech, he announced his inevitable decision to resign from the chairmanship of the CIR.

The new Act had broken the basic contention of the British Unions, namely that the voluntary system of collective bargaining was the best and fairest possible system and that any body of law would by necessity and by tradition prove to be punitive for the unions.

There were many aspects of the 1971 Act that I personally found to be unacceptable, just as there were other provisions that I regarded as unrealistic. In the main though, I took the view that the voluntarist case for reform was finished.

Rightly or wrongly, public contempt for the disruptive effects of strikes, and the strong public belief that the country's economic welfare was being endangered by the high level of industrial conflict, could no longer be ignored. Ironically it was unfortunate for the unions that the 1971 Act was just before its time, and the unions had every historical justification for their suspicion of the law. In a democratic society laws need the broad acceptance of those they govern, and union opposition to the Act made its continued existence improbable. With hindsight a leading union official recently argued that given its continued existence through the past twenty-plus years, the 1971 Act would have served the unions well. They would certainly have been better served by the 1971 provisions than by the laws that followed in the '80s.

I took on a number of interesting cases for the CIR under the 1971 provisions, including the reports which legitimized the closed shop arrangements in Marine Transport and in the Theatre. I travelled to six European countries to work on a major report entitled *Worker Participation and Collective Bargaining in Europe*, which covered all six countries. There were many other cases, but the most significant of the recognition references began in a tiny factory in Woking. It brought about a national strike in the engineering industry and in its conclusion thrust me personally into an interesting confrontation with Ministers.

The ConMech saga

In the labour law history books the ConMech case is a significant event in the short life of the National Industrial Relations Court (NIRC). The case had a strong element of farce about it and provided a dramatic example of the way in which the 1971 Act could magnify the most insignificant dispute and turn it into a political crisis. But then, in truth, so much of English law is born out of similar small events.

The ConMech case occurred against a background of legal action against trade unions for being in breach of various provisions of the Act they had chosen to ignore. The majority of TUC unions had determined that, in opposing the legislation, they would de-register, thereby excluding themselves from any benefits, and more significantly any legal immunity, which the Act might have extended to them. The majority of employers and certainly the big employers wanted no more than to get on with their business, and therefore came to an understanding with their unions, skillfully avoiding the traps laid by the legislation. But individuals and individualistic small employers were not so restrained. ConMech and its owner fell into this latter category.

The company was small, employing no more than 60, though it was a very profitable enterprise run from the top in a tough, paternalistic style. The plant had an odd production mix: on the heavy engineering side manufacturing large earth clearance and scraping blades for site leveling. On the other side of a wall of stacked oil drums, a small continuous production line (staffed by women) manufactured small blades for bread-slicing machines.

The heavy engineering work tended to be hard and dirty and in that middle-class commuter town of Woking the factory faced a constant recruitment problem. The ConMech director found a solution to this problem when he heard of a mushroom farm at Chobham going out of business. By some mysterious process the farm had managed to import and employ Sicilian and Southern Italian agricultural labourers and these were recruited *en bloc* into the ConMech factory. At first the arrangement seems to have posed few problems for the company. The men were not of a tradition to complain. With little understanding of the English language and with an even vaguer comprehension of British conventions they were unlikely to be able to articulate any complaints. In some ways the men had been well treated by the company; many had acquired substantial mortgages in Woking through the good offices of the company and with the support of the local priest. No enforcement of overtime occurred but the factory remained open for 14 or 15 hours a day and the men were at liberty to work those hours if they chose to do so. A large mortgage probably acted as adequate inducement without company pressure.

The whole arrangement seems to have worked in a most satisfactory manner as far as the company was concerned, until the owner took a fateful decision in the summer of 1972. He provided, at their request, a vacation job for two adult graduates, I seem to remember, from Warwick University. The two claimed to be appalled by the conditions under which the Italians seemed contentedly to labour over their 12 to 15 hour days. The students paid a quick visit to the local office of the Engineering Union (AUEW), obtaining a membership card for each worker and then announced themselves to the owner as the accredited shop stewards. He immediately threw them out of the factory. The two reported this back to the union and then picketed the factory with the union's blessing.

As the Italians left the factory later that night the two picketing students persuaded many not to return to work. The company then faced a real problem. Some organization, possibly a trade association, advised the owner of ConMech to seek an injunction from the NIR Court and from there the case leapt into national prominence. It was at this point that we were drawn into events.

The Court, under Sir John Donaldson, agreed to a restraining order against the union, but on the condition that the CIR would conduct a survey to determine whether the union should be granted recognition. This prospect horrified the company owner. But in a skillfully engineered private session, in which I participated, the judge pressured the company into accepting that I should move into the factory the following day. As a final retort the company director warned me that the majority of workers on the heavy engineering side spoke no English. Judge Donaldson raised his eyebrows to us. The Commission secretary and I agreed to the condition for our involvement and we then rushed back to complete the work on the questionnaires and, most of all, to find an interpreter. One of my colleagues located a Sicilian nun in the Italian hospital and, for a brief moment, I thought of the fun of arriving with a nun in full flowing habit. At the last moment, however, the Italian institute rang to confirm that they could provide a skilled interpreter, though we would not be able to meet with him until our arrival at the factory.

On a warm October morning I sat with the interpreter on a boundary wall alongside the factory. I ran through the procedure and posed the questions we needed to put to the people we intended to interview. Of all the questions one crucial one would provide the foundation for the Commission's decision. This posed the issue of whether the candidate wished to be represented by a trade union, but it was essential to emphasize that there was but one union, which at that point had no lawful status. The interpreter solemnly ran through the translation to the question and announced that it would be correct to enquire whether the worker would "wish to be represented by the *Syndicato Mafiosi*'" To put the issue in that way to Italian workers seemed at least to be a little questionable. I arranged for a telephone call to the Labour Attaché in Rome and brought him into the discussion. He confirmed the interpreter's translation as correct. I went ahead and privately posed the question to each worker and in turn they confirmed their almost universal assent.

God only knows where those people are now – probably running their own factories or a chain of restaurants in London, but at that time they had all the characteristics of peasants. Their strong features were reminiscent of a Brueghel painting, but their eyes betrayed real fear. We were gentle and friendly with them, but from their perspective these officials from government would surely begin to question how they came to be in the country. That issue was not part of my remit, however.

On my return to the Commission that evening I had a request to attend an informal late meeting at the Department of Employment, where they had maintained a close interest in the progress of the case. Already the NIR Court had sequestered £75,000 of the union's funds as a penalty for ignoring the court order to call off the ConMech strike, which at that time had no more than a dozen workers in support. At the Department I ran through the sequence of events and outlined the results of the survey: two bargaining units, but little union support among the women bread knife workers, though solid support among the heavy labourers. I advised them that my report to the Commission would lead to a recommendation for union recognition rights for part of the workforce. How long, I was asked, would it take to write the reports? Looking to a report of no more than ten pages I suggested two to three days. Ministers, I was informed, would certainly welcome a much longer gestation period for the Commission's findings.

The implication was clear. The union would continue to defy the law and suffer sequestration of its funds until it was crippled as an example for the rest of the TUC unions. I wrote the first draft of the ConMech report over the weekend and presented it to the Commission Secretary and Chairman on Monday. We recommended recognition for the heavy engineering workshop, but with the union de-registered the report was unenforceable and the employer simply ignored its findings. The court went on to

Donovan and After | 49

fine the union again, and this time compensated the company, despite the company's refusal to implement the Commission's recommendations.

In the final stage the union called a series of national strikes, with support from some newspaper workers. By this time only five stalwarts were left on the original ConMech picket line, while the court and the union battled it out at the considerable expense of the rest of the engineering industry. With the whole engineering industry in chaos the employers stepped in and dealt a crucial blow against the legal provisions. A group of major employers persuaded the court to allow them to pay the union's fine and wisely the court agreed. The union also backed away from the confrontation. The 1971 Act was virtually finished from that point.

The 1971 Act had been aesthetically commendable. It had a comprehensive form, which whetted the appetites of lawyers, and it had the litigious-minded pouring through its provisions in admiration. In practical terms the Act offered much to unions and employers alike, but it was before its time and proved to be a costly mistake. The battle over the introduction of law into British industrial relations practice had to be fought, but the government had made the mistake of believing that they would have the employers on their side in that battle. At that time unions and employers alike were opposed to the law's encroachment into their business.

A few years later the climate had changed. Employers had shed their distrust of the law and enthusiastically supported the provisions introduced by another Conservative government which, in an endeavour to confine the unions, applied layers of penalties and restrictions on them. The law is now fully engaged in the organization of trade unions and in the process of collective bargaining, but in a generally punitive style. It would be interesting to see the reaction of trade union leaders were a government to blow the dust off the 1971 Act, polish it to suit the times and challenge the unions with that balance of rights and obligations which characterized that fateful and short-lived piece of legislation.

Naturally, during the period of its involvement with the 1971 Act the CIR had faced the public hostility of the unions. Employers for the most part were none too happy to see us around their premises either. Typically though, as George Woodcock had predicted, the public position of the unions rarely debarred 'informal' discussion with union leaders where one of our inquiries affected their interests.

In 1974, the Heath government fell in the midst of the coal strike, and the incoming Labour government quickly set out to repeal the 1971 Act and abolish the CIR. Persuaded principally by Jack Jones, the government turned its attentions to the development of a conciliation and arbitration service, which had more coherence in its services and a degree more independence than had been traditionally provided by the Employment Department's conciliation officer and his staff.

At the CIR those of us who had served through the two distinct periods of its existence were sad to see it close. It had engaged a talented staff, its inquiries were thorough and its reports were totally committed to the principle that collective bargaining is the best possible way to determine the pay and conditions of people at work. We argued the case for retention with Ministers but the government had its sights set on a new panacea for our continuing industrial relations disruption. In any case with a minority position in the House the Labour government needed the support of every trade union sponsored MP.

The closure of the CIR also ended the practical influence of the Donovan Report. When the door closed on the Gower Street office of the CIR it also closed on that liberal approach to the reform of our labour relations system. I therefore left the CIR as an established civil servant, a status that would eventually qualify me for the Diplomatic Service.

Civil Service

Four Civil Service

The Miners' Strike

The Miners' strike of 1972 and 1973, during which the Conservative government fell from office, has been well documented. The government took the confrontation as a challenge to its constitutional authority and the government lost. The previous Miners' strike in 1972, which had led to the Wilberforce inquiry, had inflated both the wages and the confidence of the miners. With OPEC restructuring Middle East oil output, the economic value of home-produced coal increased and the miners were in no mood to accept government imposed restrictions on wage negotiations.

In response to the economic crisis of 1971 and 1972, the Heath government introduced a complex pay restraint policy which sought to impose pay restrictions, at first in the public sector, and then to all areas of employment. To oversee the policy the government established both a Pay Board and a Prices Commission, which looked to assist in the regulation of both pay and price movements. Derek Robinson and I were functionally close in 1973 in the dramatic events spinning out from the Heath government's counter-inflation bill and the consequent downward pressure on pay.

That 1973 Heath Government had a severe energy crisis, with OPEC quadrupling the price of oil and the Arab states restricting oil production. Then the miners, sensing their increased strength, imposed an overtime ban. In the midst of this energy and financial crisis the Government decided to establish an independent pay board. This was seen as a copy of a board established by Richard Nixon in America. The Government required the Board to advise on all those issues that inevitably arise when pay restrictions are imposed – the anomalies that arise, the special cases that emerge and the relativities in pay levels that are the drivers in pay dissatisfaction. This was exactly Derek's territory and there was nobody better qualified in that field. I had a call from the Permanent Secretary, Conrad Heron, to ask whether I thought that Derek would take the post of Deputy Chairmanship of that Pay Board if offered. If I thought that he would, then I was requested to call him. The job would only be offered of course if the answer was yes. Derek did agonise a bit over the political aspects of the job, but finally agreed. The Guardian headlined the report of his appointment with the phrase "Heath's Robinson". With the Pay Board newly established the government then sent it the miners' pay issue as a 'special reference'. Derek took on the Chairmanship of that inquiry.

Derek proved to be brilliant in that role, but I often wondered, with the extraordinary events that quickly followed his appointment, the intense media spotlight on him and the fall of the Heath government, if he wondered whether he should have shot the messenger. I can testify to the immense admiration of all involved in those events for Derek's relentless pursuit of the truth and then his determination to declare that truth. In the midst of the Miners' strike, the imposition of the three-day working week for everybody and an election campaign under way, all attention focused on the findings of the Pay Board and the young, furiously intelligent Oxford academic with a dad still working in the coal industry.

Derek always told the story of his very first day on arriving at the inquiry. During the three-day working week, with severe restrictions on all energy use, the Civil Service rule on the use of cars led to his travel in a small mini. He arrived at the inquiry at exactly the same time as the mining delegation which, unrestricted, arrived in two Daimlers. He used this event to good effect during his inquiry. I saw Derek in the middle of the process and was astonished at his confidence and stability. Fred Bayliss, the Senior Civil Servant at the Pay Board, said that Derek's questioning, conducted entirely on his own, went on for two weeks, and was forensically precise and intellectually commanding. It was a process that proved beyond doubt that none of the managers involved at any level understood the substance of their payments system. Similarly his interrogation proved that the people who best understood the pay system were those who were subject to it. Derek's interrogation process clearly left the people interrogated by him in no doubt as to their success, or not, in persuading the Pay Board of the substance of their argument. They could have had no illusions following their session responding to Derek.

Industrial relations were subject to intense public scrutiny at that time. The Financial Times had half a dozen industrial correspondents on its payroll and all the other newspapers had at least one principal industrial writer reporting on any issue to do with pay bargaining. These industrial reporters were highly skilled and adroit observers of the collective bargaining process. The Employer representative and the Union officials who were providing evidence to the Board inquiry faced a daily barrage of questions from reporters following their submissions. These were seasoned industrial relations reporters who managed to work out which way the results were likely to go and then expressed their judgments in front page predictions. The Pay Board, subject to purdah rules, decided that their report should not appear until after the election. The newspapers, on the other hand, working with their own assessments, headlined ahead of time the rejection of the Coal Board and the government's case days before polling in the election took place.

Fred Bayliss, speaking in 2015, exonerated Derek from any blame in the question of leaking the Board's inquiry. He said that no report could have held the direction of its thinking in such an intense atmosphere, with such experienced reporters watching every move and listening to every question. I talked also in 2015 to the Permanent Secretary in charge of the Department at the time,

Conrad Heron, and he was absolutely certain that the newspaper articles were unrelated to any comments that Derek might have made to the reporters. He is quite clear that Derek behaved impeccably and correctly. Conrad celebrated his 99th birthday the day after I talked to him, but he remained very sharp and with excellent recall of events during that period.

Derek believed that Heath blamed him for bringing down the government. As the newspapers were filled with predictions, Heath wrote a strong complaint to the Board Chairman, Frank Figgures, about non-attributable briefings from the Board. Then following the election and his defeat, he wrote a rather gracious apology. In Heath's biography he comments on the events and blames unnamed officials on the Board; on sober reflection he should have understood that it was the system, not Derek, that had failed him. He should also have listened to his Permanent Secretary, who told him that he had misjudged this matter.

Following these dramatic Pay Board events, Derek went on to serve in other public service positions, and worked all over the world for the ILO. He also re-kindled his teaching career at Magdalen College Oxford, enjoying the engagement with his intelligent up-and-coming students.

Visiting America

During my time at the CIR I made an interesting visit to the United States. The CIR chairman had an arrangement to visit Washington and it was thought prudent to have an official accompany him. He talked at the National Press Club and we visited various employment and labour relations organizations. At the American Federation of Labor (AFL–CIO) I had the first of many subsequent meetings with its long serving President, the redoubtable George Meany. We were some years later to be engaged together in an interesting political exercise. After Washington I went on to Chicago to visit the International Harvester plant at Melrose Park, where an old United Auto Workers organizer told me stories of his days with Walter and Victor Reuther and his recollections of the political activist Wyndam Mortimer, a relative of Jim Mortimer who became the first chairman of the Advisory, Conciliation and Arbitration Service (ACAS).

Though I had visited the States on previous occasions, this particular visit simply whetted the appetite and I cannot think of a single year since 1973 when I have failed, in one capacity or another, to spend some time in North America. In 1975 I lectured at a conference at McGill in Quebec with Hugh Clegg and Bill (later Lord) McCarthy and then in 1976 Anne Armstrong, the US Ambassador in London, kindly offered a month-long study programme in the States. Geraldine joined me for the second two weeks of that programme, which took us from Washington right across to the West Coast with six stops and programmes of visits along the way. It was during that memorable tour that I determined to do all I could to be appointed to the Washington Embassy as its Labour Counsellor. That appointment, if achieved would provide a priceless opportunity to study, in some considerable depth, the US social structures and labour market economy.

The London-bound commuter

From the now abolished CIR I had the luck to be selected as one of the few to transfer across to the new Advisory Conciliation and Arbitration Service which, alongside the abolition of the 1971 Act, the 1974 Labour Government had established as the cornerstone of its labour reforms.

One immediate personal consequence of that move was that I therefore continued to spend some two hours each way in a tedious daily journey to Westminster. After a local bus journey to Grays Station I would then take the train to Fenchurch Street and from there go by Tube to Westminster. The Southend line at that time held an unassailable position as the most strike-ridden and unreliable in the country. The carriages were spartan and dirty, and sprung for full loads, so that on late night journeys home in empty carriages we suffered every conceivable shock to the spinal system. On journeys into London we were packed together in a standing, swaying mass of sweating humanity, finding the luxury of a seat on one day in ten at the most.

For a blessed short time I found a welcome relief from this daily torture. An enterprising fellow purchased two splendid East German hydrofoil vessels to run a service along the Thames from Gravesend to Westminster Pier. The price seemed a bit high but the journey had both comfort and, depending on the light, an occasional touch of magnificence. The journey to London was swift and smooth and with the sun rising behind us we were frequently greeted by a London glistening in its reflections along the river. As we skimmed along, coffee would be served and our choice of newspaper delivered to the seat. It was a commuter service unparalleled by any other I have subsequently encountered anywhere in the world. Sadly the magic faded in a series of mishaps on numerous return journeys.

At that time the Thames still attracted a healthy commercial traffic along its length to the Royal Docks and much of it still carried conventional cargo. Naturally the tides among it carried a heavy mixture of debris which moved back and forth along the length of the river. On one occasion during an evening return home we lost a hydrofoil float thanks to a drifting plank of timber. On another return to Gravesend, a length of nylon rope wound around one of our propeller shafts and burned it to a solid block with the friction.

On the occasion of an accident the vessel would slump into the water and continue its journey, but in the style of an old barge. On such evenings the journeys home were very long and we invariably arrived at our destination much worse for the enforced period spent in the vessel's evening bar room.

When the hydrofoil ceased its service, defeated by river flotsam, I had no alternative but to return to the train. Watching commuters on that line one could regularly gain the impression that the whole population was gripped by a collective madness, or alternatively subscribed to some grey flannel religious cult that encouraged mass suicide. Each weekday morning passengers would arrive at the station to hear the whistle of the station guard and the increasing rumble of the train's accelerating engine. A pack of commuters would sprint alongside the speeding train, open carriage doors and throw themselves into the opening. Arriving home, while the returning train still sped at high, though decelerating speed, every carriage door would be thrown open and bodies would lean out in anticipation. At the crucial moment, with the train still at speed, they would leap as one from every carriage and hit the platform, propelled forward at three times the speed they would normally run unaided.

On one morning trip to London I joined in the fun and sprinted for the departing train. I wore a brand new pair of shoes and, leaping into the carriage, I was assisted by a helpful fellow who pulled the carriage door closed, unfortunately trapping my foot. My left shoe then fell from my foot and, I later discovered, deposited itself on the gravel alongside the track. Next stop Fenchurch Street. The other occupants in the carriage just ignored my plight and not a word passed between us. In London the rain fell heavily and along the road large puddles made progress in my wet sock a little hazardous. At the taxi rank a jolly driver welcomed me with the consoling thought that in the dull routine of his life there was always one who made his day. I had clearly been nominated to that position.

"Where do you wish to go now?" he asked. Obviously to a shoe shop, so I gave him directions to a store that I knew would stock my esoteric size. Then came the challenge. He pulled the cab over somewhere along Holborn, turned to face me and offered to split the cab fare if I were to go into the store and very seriously ask the assistant to provide a single shoe to match the one on my right foot. It seemed a fair deal to me. Just after nine o'clock on a rainy Monday morning on the corner of Holborn and Kingsway a man wearing only one shoe entered the shoe shop, faced the assistant and solemnly requested a single shoe to match the one he was wearing. The assistant seemed a little perplexed and then patiently explained that shoes always came in pairs (and his face betrayed his innermost thoughts – "What a way to start a week!").

"But", said the customer, "are you suggesting that an unfortunate accident victim with one leg would be forced by you to purchase twice as many shoes as he needed?" The assistant nodded but his eyes furtively looked around for hidden cameras. Outside, the taxi driver grinned through the window behind the assistant and held up his thumbs. As I left the store I realized that the assistant had at no time betrayed any curiosity as to the circumstances that had led to my problem. Maybe it was a fairly common occurrence!

A conciliatory time

The 1974 Labour government speedily introduced a law to restore union freedoms to some extent as they had been before the 1971 Act. Then, one year later, a 1975 Act dignified ACAS with a legal 'independence' that unions had claimed to be necessary for the effective functioning of third party intervention into collective bargaining. The Act laid down that the service could not be subject to directions of any kind by a Minister. That statute gave the service not only the duty to reform the collective bargaining process, but a specific duty to promote it. It seemed self-evident to me that the duty to extend collective bargaining was not a task that would fit easily on the shoulders of the old style conciliators in the Department. They were bred in the comfortable tradition of splitting the difference, but the recognition decisions on collective bargaining made by a statutory body were quasi-judicial and could not be massaged into reality.

The solution to this dilemma could have been straightforward, and Jack Jones seemed to be the first to articulate the case. The service should be staffed by non-civil servants drawn from all areas of employment. This would have reflected the staffing of the CIR and the successful way that both the FMCS and the NLRB in the United States traditionally organize their staff. This still leaves the chairmanship and board members to be appointed by Ministers.

The Civil Service unions were not at all happy with this proposition and demanded the opportunity to address the ACAS Board. Jack Jones as a board member asked them a simple question:

"Are you affiliated to the TUC?". They said yes, and all Jack's arguments evaporated and with it, in my view the essential independence of mind that the civil service needed.

The ACAS workforce was not at one with the task the statute had entrusted to them. I had to stomp the country, address meetings of ACAS staff and lay out the procedure for conducting recognition cases. This recognition work was not a task that suited either their temperament or the role they had sought to play within their local communities. Many were longstanding members of Rotary Clubs or Chambers of Commerce and here they were, being forced into a quasi-judicial role; being charged with the duty to foist collective bargaining on the members of the very institutions they had joined in order to establish their social credibility. It was an impossible mix. The adjudication of collective bargaining rights cannot be carried out entirely by conciliation officers. It is a question of social justice and must have its own decision-making process, its own judgmental standards and its own staff. For my part, though, there were other, achievable tasks in ACAS. The Royal Commission on the Press passed over to ACAS the duty to examine the collective bargaining practices in both the national and the regional press. It was a mammoth task and with a strict deadline. The national study put us into Fleet Street for almost a year, interviewing all the managers at every newspaper and, working through many nights, every shop steward.

The resulting ACAS National Press Report is a densely detailed analysis of the previously obscured processes of collective bargaining at each of the national newspapers. In fact the whole newspaper collective bargaining process was corrupt and based on long-standing practices designed to apply workgroup pressure on the proprietors at their most vulnerable moments. Over many years the proprietors, principally interested in the degree to which they could use the newspaper to influence and impress government, had given in to workgroup pressure in order to bring out their editions on time. As a result the industry carried the burden of labour overmanning. It worked with obsolete machinery and its management typically had to wrestle with not one, but many convoluted payment systems that jointly carried within them the autonomous motivation to inflate wages continuously.

I look back on that ACAS report to the Royal Commission with some considerable regret. The whole of the national newspaper industry possibly needed to suffer the challenge of an Eddie Shah on new technology. It may also have needed to go through the battle with Rupert Murdoch and his move of the Times to the high technology plant at Wapping. Leaving aside the complex arguments on both sides, I do believe that the ACAS National Press Report typifies the weakness of the institution in that it could not possibly face up to the harsh truth about the unacceptable nature of labour practices in the industry. It is the fact of the matter that we lost the opportunity to describe the reality of the situation and then challenge the shop floor labour practices that were crippling the industry. The Fleet Street print unions were riddled with malpractice: the employers had handed effective management of their plant over to the unions. After a year in Fleet Street we had the evidence to produce a report that might have stood a chance of initiating reform. The failure to achieve that left the battle with the unions to be brutally pushed through by proprietors Eddie Shah and then Rupert Murdoch.

Diplomatic Credentials

Five Diplomatic Credentials

Washington DC

The opportunity to go to the Washington Embassy as Labour Counsellor came much quicker than I had anticipated. We departed without much time to ponder the implications but with great excitement at the prospect, though not before the foreign Labour Attachés in London hosted a dinner to welcome me as one of their kind. Alyce came with us, but Steven departed to begin his degree course on the day we left for America. I felt terribly guilty abandoning him that way and it was upsetting to see him walking along the road with his backpack as we loaded the luggage for our departure to the airport. He subsequently spent more time in America during the first two years of his degree than he did in England.

We arrived in Washington during a very hot October and set about searching for a house to rent. With the assistance of a realtor I looked around at one or two, then the agent urged us to visit a house just off MacArthur Boulevard which she indicated was owned by an American State Department official. It suited us fine. On moving in day we waited around for our possessions to come from the UK. Impatient, by 7 pm we were setting off to find somewhere to eat. Driving along MacArthur Boulevard to Georgetown a truck approached with large letters painted on a container reading PETER D. CARR, WASHINGTON. We reversed and drove back to the house to be greeted by four jovial black members of the Teamsters Union ready to unload. We moved in to 5220$^{1/2}$, which was tucked in between two older houses. The house was furnished and over the dining table hung a chandelier with an intriguing ochre colour. On closer examination we realized the glass on the chandelier had a fine coating of some substance. We found other indications of the previous occupants with wiring for long distance radio transmission, and a negative of a Kurdish tribesman dressed in full battle gear. Our Foreign Office neighbours two doors away explained that the previous occupant of the house was General Mustafa Barzani, the military leader of the Kurds. The coating on the chandelier came from his hookah pipe and the photograph was of his son Masoud, who today leads the Kurds. Mustafa Barzani had been in Washington for cancer treatment and died soon after we arrived. To thank the Americans he had presented the President with a large circular rug, and it was interesting to note that the rug features in photographs in the State Department during Masoud Barzani's visit to Washington in 2014. It intrigues us to know that for four and a half years in Washington we slept in the same bed as Mustafa Barzani. In the spring following our arrival, during Steve's visit he explored our garden. Clutching handfuls of a plant he asked why we were growing cannabis. We suspected it was one of the products that went into the hookah pipe.

The Labour Counsellor's job in Washington hadn't changed much since the first one took up his post in 1941. Professor R.H. Tawney went to Washington that year to assist the Ambassador, Lord Halifax, to get close to the Democratic New Deal politicians and to develop an understanding of labour movement policies. The Foreign Secretary in 1941, Anthony Eden, had expressed his concern about the somewhat fractious division between the two arms of the American Labour Movement, the AFL and the CIO, a division which some believed to be capable of disrupting the manufacturing industry and consequently the flow of military supplies to Britain.

When Tawney arrived in Washington neither of us had a brief for the job ahead. Like myself, he had also arrived burdened with the task of finding a house to rent. His role set him somewhat apart from the Foreign Office professionals, as did mine. But the United States I served in was not that of Tawney's day. When I arrived I found a country undergoing a crisis of confidence. The belief in the limitless nature of resources, in the capacity of man to solve all problems and the confident drive of individual Americans to succeed through their own endeavours was by no means as pronounced a part of the national character as it had been 10 or 15 years before. It was, of course, still a land of immense wealth, populated by an energetic, friendly and often appealingly naive people. It still had a vigorous economy. It was a vast nation, much of it waiting for development and ready to absorb the rapidly growing population. In 1978, the year of my arrival in Washington, the nation's population grew by almost two million and the country absorbed that growth with little economic difficulty.

There were also less attractive sides to American life, which it was easy for a short-term visitor to overlook. A diplomat, even one concerned with labour relations and social affairs, could remain only vaguely conscious of the darker side of the nation. During my time in America over 20,000 people each year died from criminal activity. Over 400,000 Americans were locked in prisons and over one million were on probation or parole. Rather more than one thousand convicts awaited execution. A lot of crime was rooted in the poverty to be seen just beyond the glittering Capitol building in Washington. Over 20% of Washington residents had incomes below the official poverty line. Over 100,000 of the city's residents qualified to receive food stamps. In the 1980s almost 60% of all babies born to Washington DC residents were to single mothers and the infant mortality rate of 27.3 per 100 was as high as the rate for many impoverished developing nations.

Living as I did, like most diplomats on the Northwest side of the city, it was easy to ignore the fact that Washington was a black town. Over 70% of DC residents were black, but when Tawney worked there over 65% had been white. As the middle class moved out they took with them their high taxable incomes and their children. The town had 78 totally black schools and 15 others with only two or three white pupils. All the schools were desperately short of funding. When the kids left, or more likely dropped out of the city schools there were few jobs for them. Over 65% of the city's teenagers were unemployed. In truth they found employment in the underground economy.

There was, and still is, a very creditable side to the capital's education system. Seven universities exist in the town and two had a mainly black enrolment. From these institutions many determined black students have graduated to middle-class occupations and an archetypal middle-class American lifestyle. This newly emerging generation of middle class African-Americans will as surely change the style of the American political system as they have changed the politics of the capital city.

The American trade unions had been the staple diet of British Labour Counsellors appointed to the Washington Embassy since Tawney arrived there in 1941. American unions, never popular as mass movements, were distinctively out of favour by the late 1970s. But unions had more severe problems than their ratings in public esteem. By the 1980s unemployment tended to be at its most severe in the industries where the unions had their strongest base and the American Labour Movement suffered an erosion of its power base. However, the failure of the US unions to recruit new members went back beyond the 1980s unemployment. From 1970 to 1980 the United States economy grew at a rate unmatched by any modern society. Twenty-one million jobs were added in those 10 years but union membership stuck at 22 million – some 21% of the labour force. This failure to ride the rise in new jobs had a complex of causes. US Labor Law certainly did not help the union efforts to recruit and organize in new technology industries. The National Labor Relations Act (NLRA) excludes supervisors and anyone with managerial responsibilities from the statutory provisions covering union elections, and the newer industries had a relatively high proportion of managerial and a lower proportion of manual staff. The predominating ethos in America puts a high value on individual effort and individual acquisitiveness, which fits uncomfortably with the collectivist nature of union organization.

George Meany

I had talked with George Meany, President of the AFL–CIO, on two occasions prior to my arrival in Washington as a member of the diplomatic corps. Then on my first day in the Embassy I had a call from George Meany's factotum son-in-law, Ernie Lee, to ask if I would see Mr Meany that day. "What does he want?" seemed a necessary question. He would like, said Ernie, to discuss the deal between the British government and the TUC on incomes policy. He wanted to know what the unions believed they would get out of the deal.

My books and papers were still packed— so I had memory only to guide me in the discussion. George had a rocking chair in the style of President Kennedy's chair. He began by recalling our previous meeting and then probed my background. I thought it wise (with an ex-New York plumber) to begin at the beginning and emphasize my construction industry experience. At that time I was still a member of the Woodworkers Union, though by then it had merged with the bricklayers. As Clive Jenkins constantly pointed out I had the distinction of being the only member of the British Diplomatic Service to hold such a union card. It proved invaluable in that meeting with George Meany and in many other subsequent encounters.

"What is it", George Meany asked, "that persuades the British unions to hold back their wage demands within this incomes policy deal?" I ran him through the background and explained the union interest in expanding their role over management decision making, through a form of worker participation. There were other incentives and I took him through them.

When I had finished he had a few extra questions, quite precise ones and clearly based on good pre-briefing. Then he thanked me for the discussion. For my part I hazarded to enquire whether he would tell me why he needed to know about the British situation. He rose from the rocking chair and waved me over to the window with his stick. The AFL–CIO building on 16th Street gives its leader a priceless overlooking view of the White House below.

"Down there"' said Mr Meany, "is a little bastard who has asked to see me in half an hour. He [the President of the United States] has visited your Prime Minister Callaghan, has a suit woven with the same initials, JC, and he now wants a deal with the American labor unions to curb wage inflation on the pattern of the British deal. When I see him I will now know what to say. If I ask for the same deal the British unions have achieved, the President will walk away," he said with a grin.

I was pretty horrified by this response. I had no remit to interfere in American politics, but here, on my first day in Washington, I had walked into an involvement in a crucial negotiation between the President of the United States and the American Labor Movement. I was nonetheless intrigued by the bitterness of Meany's language. This after all was a Democratic President and by tradition he should have enjoyed a good measure of support from the Federation. It was a crucial weakness of Carter that he did not have that support. Less than a year before the ensuing Presidential elections I watched Carter address the delegates to the AFL–CIO Congress, but his address followed a stinging attack made on him by Meany from the same platform a few hours before.

Carter, in Meany's eye, had one fatal flaw – he was not Jack Kennedy. But even with that fault, Carter could have won the old man over by following the practice of other Democratic Presidents and calling Meany occasionally on the telephone. In a system without permanent political organizations, the AFL–CIO political action committees can provide a vital organizational structure for a Democratic candidate, so long as that candidate makes clear by his actions and words that he is not a creature of their making. Meany had demonstrated his own and the Federation's political power in 1972 when, in reaction to policy and procedure changes in the Democratic Party, he moved the AFL–CIO into a neutral position. Richard Nixon's election victory owed a great deal to that action by Meany. Before I left him on that first day of my diplomatic career, George Meany tapped me on the shoulder and asked: "Do you know what this man (the President) has done to the American worker? He has caused a massive price rise in the staple diet of American workers. The price of hamburgers is now beyond their reach." It was no joke.

It was on a later visit to my home in Washington that George Meany first indicated his intention to return the AFL–CIO to membership of the International Confederation of Free Trade Unions (ICFTU) and at the same time to persuade the new Reagan Administration of the necessity to return to the ILO. The United States had walked out of the ILO arguing that both the United Nations, and in turn the ILO, had abused the principles of 'due process' which should have applied to a debate on the question of Israel's treatment of the Palestinians. The American Unions had departed from the ICFTU over a similar issue in 1963. Though the US government felt little effect from the ILO withdrawal, by contrast the American Union Federation began to sense that it had suffered an increasing isolation in its detachment from the ICFTU.

The British government line tended to be somewhat different, depending on the view of the particular department. The Foreign Office tended to float above such technical questions, but more pragmatic views from the Employment Department strongly argued in favour of assisting the movement of the Americans back into the international arena. Many British unions had firmly established links with eastern European labour federations, which formed channels of annual visits to capitals in Communist countries to the east of Berlin. These boozy, cloistered trips to the havens of working-class culture provided annual injections of support for dotty left wing politics in TUC conferences and more seriously within the Labour Party. The British government took the view that, while it might question the form and activity of the ICFTU and the ILO, any move which implied a drift towards a more isolationist America should be countered and if possible avoided. If the AFL–CIO could be persuaded to return to the ICFTU and from that the US government return to its seat in the ILO, then America would be playing its full part in the international agenda. That move might, at the same time, act to inhibit the two-way union traffic between Britain and Eastern Europe. It was my brief to encourage the Americans to move back into the international organizations.

In a meeting at the International Club, Henry Kissinger privately indicated to me that the American government's decision to move back into full membership of the ILO would be contingent on George Meany's decision to let the AFL–CIO resume its role in the ICFTU. I held a number of informal meetings with George Meany and his staff on various subjects and wherever possible I raised the question of the union's return to the ICFTU. In dealing with the Americans on the question of a return to the ICFTU, and particularly in the case of George Meany, I had to be keenly aware of the long and contentious history that had led them to their position on the outside rather than the inside of that international organization. In the mid 1950's, Meany generally supported a close involvement with the ICFTU. This was on the rather negative grounds that any weakening of its structure could persuade some union federations, from for example, Africa and South America, to link up with the communist-dominated World Federation of Trade Unions (WFTU). Meany did not trust the judgement of the ICFTU leaders, particularly in their support for trade union educational programmes in third world countries. Meany was working at that time to set up international organizations in three global regions that would deliver programmes reflecting 'American values'. The AFL part of the American Federation generally supported Meany's analysis and action, but the CIO part of the Federation, under the leadership of Walter Reuther the autoworkers leader, strongly supported the ICFTU and were deeply suspicious of Meany's construction of international development bodies outside it.

The culture of the two wings of the American Federation was diverse – the AFL was deeply traditional and militantly anticommunist, having an historic base in the craft unions. The CIO, on the other hand, was more liberal, concerned with organizing industries and confident enough in its own convictions to be willing to engage in dialogue with the East Europeans and the Russians. Neither Walter Reuther, nor his brother Victor, whom

Diplomatic Credentials | 69

I knew well, were enamoured by the Soviet system, having had direct experience of working there. As young men they had cycled across Europe in 1934 and continued by train into Russia, where they had worked at the Gorky car production plant for 18 months.

The ICFTU had been formed in 1949 from union federations withdrawing from the WFTU after severe disagreement with the communist unions, mainly those from Eastern Europe. The main prompters of the split were the AFL-CIO and the British unions. Having established the ICFTU, the AFL-CIO then withdrew in 1969. This followed Walter Reuther's independent application for his United Auto-Workers Union to join the ICFTU following his union's departure from the AFL-CIO. Once outside the ICFTU, George Meany acquired major funding from the US Department of State for his international institutions to promote union education in the three regions of Africa, South America and the Far East. He also received money from American corporate businesses that supported the development. One needed to have all of this background history in mind when dealing with George Meany on the subject of the ICFTU. It was a subject that still opened up old wounds, stirred up old tensions and encouraged the formation of the old battle lines. The approach had to be sensitive to all of this.

AFL–CIO and the TUC

George enjoyed visits to our home and whenever British union officers came to Washington we made a show of the event and invited the US labour leader to join us. On one such visit, after the others had left, I posed the question to Meany as he sat in my rocking chair: When would the Federation rejoin the ICFTU? He grinned and replied: "This year if the British make it possible and sit down with us again." Acting on this indication I went to London to see Len Murray, the TUC General Secretary. Meany was clearly in failing health and I told Murray that the AFL–CIO relations would best be repaired while the AFL–CIO leader still lived. The two leaders had fallen out over Meany's persistent criticism of British union delegation visits to Eastern Europe.

Len Murray agreed with my suggestion that a *rapprochement* with the Americans would be an improvement on the acrimony which then existed between the Federations. Murray also agreed that a visit by British union officials to engage the American union leaders in a dialogue would be a sensible approach. Nevertheless, in its best tradition the TUC almost scuppered the whole visit by not including Murray, but Ken Gill among its delegates. Gill, the able, intelligent and popular General Secretary of TASS, the technicians' and draughtsmen's union, had one major drawback as far as the American unions were concerned: he was a longstanding member of the Communist Party. The whole delegation consequently met with a polite but somewhat distant response by the American union leaders, though individual British leaders were picked out for more cordial treatment.

One effect of Gill's inclusion was that, as a group, they never got inside the AFL–CIO headquarters. George Meany had established a principle for admission to that building some years before when Anastaz Mikoyan visited Washington as the newly elected first Deputy Premier of the Soviet Union. Mikoyan was there in the States to demonstrate the contrast between his (short-lived) deputy premiership and that of Joseph Stalin and during his visit he attempted to meet people and to initiate impromptu visits. On passing the 16th Street headquarters of the AFL–CIO he asked his hosts if he could see inside, but it happened to be Sunday. An accompanying FBI agent knocked on the glass door until a janitorial guard came to investigate. "This", said the FBI agent, "is the Deputy Premier of the Soviet Union. He wishes to see inside the foyer of the building". The janitor said that he would need to phone officials to get permission to open the door. The FBI agent interjected to advise him to go directly to Mr Meany. The message came back fairly quickly. "Mr Meany says that no damned 'Commie' will set foot in my building". And nor did Ken Gill either.

George Meany had a visceral hatred of the communist system and of anybody who represented it. Walter Reuther did meet Mikoyan for lunch during that Russian Minister's 1959 visit to

Washington in order, Reuther argued, to let Mikoyan know what the American unions thought about Russian intervention in Hungary and its action in Berlin. Meany caustically remarked that he could not understand an American who "feels they can meet the Soviet challenge at the conference table."

Even President Eisenhower failed to persuade Meany to host a meeting of his executive council to meet Nikita Khrushchev during the Soviet President's 1960 visit to San Francisco, where the AFL-CIO convention was coincidentally in session in the city. Despite the difficulties, however, the visit of British union leaders managed to establish rather better relationships between the two federations. Sometime after the visit, George Meany's condition deteriorated following a golf cart accident and I talked to Len Murray about the possibility of a meeting between the two of them. Len agreed and he came to Washington to see the by now bedridden, American labour leader.

At about 10 pm on the evening prior to the meeting, Len Murray called to suggest that it might be appropriate for him to take a gift, but that he had omitted to bring one. He had been told that Meany had a liking for Liberty ties and asked if I could locate a shop that sold them and produce one in time for his 11 am meeting the following day. Where in the name of wonder could I be certain of locating a Liberty tie? Geraldine suggested Saks Fifth Avenue store in Bethesda. The following morning I arrived there at 9 am to find that it was training day and the store would not be opening until 10.30 am. Waiting outside I waylaid a smartly dressed lady about to enter the darkened store. I explained my mission and told her of an international visitor and of Mr Meany's poor state of health. I struck lucky with my choice of candidate. She was a floor manager, a union member and a great fan of George Meany. I left the still locked shop with a Liberty tie neatly boxed and caught Len Murray just as he was leaving for the meeting. He assured me that the TUC would gratefully reimburse me the cost. I took that as a joke!

On 10 January 1980, shortly after he stepped down from the AFL–CIO Presidency, the 85-year-old George Meany died. He lay 'in state' in the 16th Street building and AFL–CIO officials persuaded Geraldine and myself that we were expected to call in to pay our final respects to the old warrior. As I looked down at that tough old man I recognized the tie: still unpaid for, but hopefully sealing a small knot in US /British relations.

For George Meany's funeral all the public buildings in Washington flew their flags at half-mast, including those around the Washington monument. On August 16, his birthday, the US post office issued a commemorative stamp and in 1994 another postage stamp carried his portrait. That may well have been a nation saying goodbye to the last of his kind; a union powerbroker with a strength that required even Presidents of the United States to stroke his ego. Longevity and long service have played their part in the power of AFL–CIO Presidents. When Lane Kirkland took over from Meany he became only the fourth AFL–CIO leader since 1886. During that same period the United States had elected nineteen Presidents to the White House.

The American unions formally decided to return to the International Confederation of Free Trade Unions at their 1979 Convention, which I attended a few months before Meany died. Responding to that decision, as Kissinger had predicted, the US government formally applied in 1980 for re-entry to the ILO.

The Labour Attaché Role

In his role as Foreign Secretary, the great Ernest Bevin gave official sanction to the appointment of Labour Attachés based in British Embassies around the World. Even China had one. In 1950, 21 of them were in place, covering over 38 separate countries, with a number of them appointed to more than one post. This stretching of their responsibilities beyond national boundaries often made for an impossible workload. For example the Labour Attaché in Egypt also dealt with Ethiopia, Iraq, Jordan, Lebanon, Libya, Saudi Arabia, Sudan and Syria.

Preceding all of that, Professor R.H. Tawney went out to Washington in 1941 at the behest of the Foreign Secretary, Anthony

Eden, to see what could be done to overcome the disputes between the two branches of the American Labour movement, the AFL and the CIO. The British view was that the disputes were seriously endangering the flow of military supplies to the British. Tawney was seen as the ideal candidate – the leading social historian of his time, no union politics associated with him and the ability to analyze the most complex problems with speed and eloquence. But an undercurrent of other reasons ran through the decision to appoint Tawney. The fact was that senior Cabinet ministers had little confidence in the qualifications of Lord Halifax, the Ambassador, to deal with this problem. Apart from his academic status, Tawney was highly regarded as an implacable opponent of appeasement – the issue which had prompted Winston Churchill to remove Halifax from London and move him to Washington in the first place. Tawney seems to have endowed the Washington post with the title of Counsellor, which continued until my time there. He felt that this title was more conciliatory and conveyed an empathy that he might usefully exploit in his work.

By the time I went to Washington the number of Labour Attachés in British embassies had been reduced to ten. Their functions, grades and the use made of them by their Home Departments differed widely. The Brussels Labour Attaché, for example, was almost solely concerned with European Commission matters and had his activities tightly controlled by his own Home Departments. The South African Attaché in Pretoria had his focus on the impact of the oppressive South African regulations on British businesses operating there. The particular Attaché during my time ran into trouble with the Foreign Office and was removed. I concluded that this was for shipping information to the States at the request of a Californian pro-civil rights lawyer – the South African Attaché was using my office as a pipeline.

Generally the British Labour Attachés came from the Employment/Labour Department though some specialists were occasionally shipped across from other Departments. Like all other specialist Attachés the Labour Attaché is under the authority of the Ambassador or Head of Mission but also serves the Ministry from which they were assigned. Washington was always regarded as the senior post and had a grade to reflect that status. For the most part Labour Attachés worked in an open and straight forward way with little covert activity. There is an obvious need to protect the integrity of information going back to the home government. The tone of reports needs to be protected as well as the content. Activity, on the other hand, that entails influencing or changing policies without openly declaring that intention might be regarded as verging on the covert. This would be rare territory for a Labour Attaché, and for the most part they are not equipped for it. Most embassies are furnished with secure rooms, suspended and protected from electronic surveillance. It is there that the most confidential issues may be discussed.

The North American activities of Noraid, the Northern Ireland fundraising organization, drew me into some heavy activity with the leadership of a number of American unions. The British government regarded Noraid, as an IRA front organization. The US Department of Justice supported that view and in 1981 it won a case against Noraid, forcing it to register the IRA as a "foreign principle". In this finding the United States District Court Judge, Charles S. Haight, wrote of "incontrovertible evidence that [Noraid] is an agent of the IRA, providing money and services for other than relief purposes." Unquestionably Noraid funds did go to some worthy causes, including vacations for Northern Ireland children, taking them away from the strife for a while. They were also the main funding agency for Belfast's Green Cross, which had a central role in maintaining an adequate prisoner relief programme. But the view in the United States Justice Department, supported by those in Northern Ireland, was that a proportion of the money collected in North America went to purchase weapons that were then shipped to the IRA. This view was later supported by trial evidence given by Michael Hanratty, a former electronics purchaser to the IRA, who said in the Brooklyn gun running trial of 1983, that "Noraid money was sent over to Northern Ireland and when equipment was to be purchased a courier then took some of the money and carried it back to this [USA] country".

American unions provided Noraid with an accessible vehicle for fundraising. Union conventions were big, and frequently allowed speakers from charities to make heart-felt appeals. Some unions, such as the Building Workers, had strong Irish/American membership and were particularly receptive. I had the task of dissuading the union leadership from allowing Noraid a platform for their activity. For that role I needed to be on very close terms with the leaders. My evidence had to be convincing and I had to be trusted to deal with them in complete confidence. But it was very tense activity.

The United States initiated its own appointment of Labour Attachés in 1943. In the post-war period political systems were reviving, while the re-established trade unions were, in some cases, even challenging established power structures. The American administration determined that its embassies should be equipped with specialist officers who could assist the Ambassadors to interpret the union and the left of centre organizations in their political activity. From the outset the US Labor Attaché core had responsibility both to interpret and quietly influence foreign labour politics. They clearly worked to further American interests, which included nurturing labour leaders and organizations that accorded with the American analysis of its friends and its foes. I knew many of the Labour Attachés in the American Embassy in London in the early 1970's, for example Herb Weiner and Harry Pollak. All of the American Attachés were international professionals and supremely well informed. They were linked to the Bureau of Foreign Labor Affairs in the US Department of State. The strength of the British unions at that time, coupled with the disruptive nature of our industrial relations system, guaranteed a high level of American interest. The US Labor Attachés were chosen for their ability to mix well with union leaders and for their astuteness in assessing the possible direction of events. They were also required to have the skills to influence. Some of the British far left regarded the Labour Attachés as CIA officers, but this was too simplistic. I knew most of the American Attachés based in London in the 60s and 70s and never judged them to be involved in covert activity. That role they could leave to others.

There are always exceptions to any general rule, and Joseph Godson was a classic exception.[3] He served as United States Labor Attaché in London from 1952-1959 and worked with considerable energy to engage in Labour Party politics, undermining the left and strengthening the right. Geoffrey Goodman, the Daily Mirror's industrial correspondent, revealed Godson's anti-Bevanite activity and claimed that Godson's Kensington flat was "a salon for Gaitskellites". Godson was also in attendance at a meeting in the Russell Hotel at which Hugh Gaitskell planned the expulsion of Nye Bevan from the Labour Party.

In Washington we had a very active group of around a dozen Labour Attachés from various embassies based there. The Swedish Labour Attaché had an oddly detached position, being nominated alternately by the Employers' Federation and the Union Federation respectively. Their Attachés were thus not subject to the authority of their Head of Mission but to their respective Federations. There is an inherent weakness in that form of structure, as the Americans found out when they introduced a range of Attachés to their larger departments at the turn of the century. The weakness of the Swedish system was demonstrated soon after my arrival in Washington. In some unrecorded way the Swedish Attaché had intensely annoyed Mr George Meany, the AFL/CIO President. The Swede was a union nominee. A call from the AFL-CIO President's office to his Swedish counterpart in Stockholm was sufficient to ensure the Attaché's departure: his Ambassador played no part in that process.

The Japanese Labour Attachés were generally young mid-career officials from their Labour Department, who worked to facilitate visits and bilateral relations between employer groups and unions in the two countries. Each country puts a distinctive stamp on the responsibilities of their Attachés. Countries have different bilateral relationships and their diplomatic missions have roles to perform that reflect these distinctions. The task of Japanese Attachés was to counter the resistance of the American unions to Japanese imports,

---

3 Harold Wilson Biography by Ramsey and Dorri

particularly cars, and then to promote the establishment of Japanese car manufacturing in the United States.

The South American Attachés in Washington had issues related to migration as a prime responsibility. I worked closely with the German Labour Attaché, Rudolph Volmer, from time to time conducting joint studies, organizing joint programmes for German and British visitors, attending White House Press conferences together and exchanging notes on events. I always felt that our reports had a special quality as a result of that co-operation, though we always acknowledged our different perspectives on issues.

From my friendship with the Japanese Attaché I learned something new about the characteristic Japanese fondness for play. We attended a reception and dinner at the Japanese Embassy to mark some significant day in the Japanese calendar. The event turned out to be very stiff, quiet and formal, but of course superbly organized with a banquet of the best Japanese food. As we arrived home after the event Geraldine realized that she had left her handbag, so dropping her at our Klingle Street house I doubled back to recover the bag. Parking at the Embassy I felt some relief that it was well lit and clearly still in entertainment mode. As I approached, the noise level seemed unusually high, the cheering and applause at a level not heard at any point during the earlier reception. On entering the Embassy area I realized that the room had taken on the form of a casino, with various games on the go and some hard drinking taking place. I was greeted with cheers and welcomed back. I arrived home very late that night.

Despite differences in the roles of the Attachés, however, the basic responsibilities and skills required were nonetheless similar. One inter-governmental organization, The International Migration Institute, has defined the prerequisites of a Labour Attaché as being diplomacy, counselling, negotiation, analytical, organizational, research, networking, data-handling, statistical and psychological assessment skills, and of course proficiency in the language of the host country. It is a fair list and accords with the demands made by the Washington job, though from my experience I would add political skills, but that may have been the nature of the post at that particular time. In my annual report of February 1981 I listed the work carried out during the year. It included programmes for 36 separate UK visitors, including the CBI President and the Secretary of State for Employment; seventeen lectures including sessions at Cornell, Stamford and Harvard, as well as seminars for the Chicago Bar Association and members of the National Association of Manufacturers. I produced 25 reports that year on subjects as diverse as employment; the social problems of black workers; changes in US employment; the history, and the trial and downfall of Tony Scotto. I also made a substantial contribution to the British government's 1981 Green paper on trade union immunities. In this I examine nine aspects of American legislation and its impact on union, employer and employee behavior.

In all of the embassies that formerly appointed British Labour Attachés that role has now disappeared. With the advance of new technologies since the 1970s a fair proportion of the 100 or so reports I produced could now be written in London, though I think they would fail to carry the conviction that first-hand engagement provides. Nonetheless with the internet some kind of report could be completed. Negotiations on labour market issues could be and now are carried out by Foreign Office staff with occasional support from specialists in home departments. The real loss though, to the Government, is in the type of information and intelligence that an effective Labour Attaché provides. That intelligence, drawn from outside the official departments and from non-governmental organizations, provides a distinct perspective that adds vitality to high-level policy assessments.

Immigrant labour

The United States had an unparalleled period of growth in the decade from the early 1970s. The employed workforce grew by 25% in that period, and in the second half of the decade over one million women each year entered the labour force. By the 1980s almost two out of every three new jobs in the economy were being filled by women.

The American dream (the prospect of constant economic growth and individual opportunity) has always attracted masses of optimistic immigrants, and the 1970s and '80s were no exception. At that time the US Labor Department believed that between seven and twelve million illegal immigrants were resident in the country and were being joined by over a million more each year.

Until the public mood changed in the 1990s, the US government applied great tolerance and a measure of calculated inefficiency in its application of immigration policy. During the 1970s and '80s the US public accepted high immigration with either benign resignation or with manipulative support. Middle class households, including our diplomatic one, employed Filipino girls as domestics without asking the obvious questions, and small employers staffed out their workforce on the minimum wage with no questions asked.

The social security tax system itself reduced the degree of public intolerance to immigrants. Before gaining employment, a prospective worker needed to obtain a social security number so that an employer could lawfully deduct the necessary social security payments from employees' wages. This protected the employer from any charge that he had knowingly employed illegal immigrant labour. In our family experience a social security number was easily obtained. No questions were asked about nationality or status in the country. This might seem strange until the implications are fully considered. The social security number leads to the deduction of contributions from wages, but does not qualify the individual for social security support. Claiming benefits on the other hand is a far more contentious process. Before any welfare is paid out, some searching questions are asked on the nationality and residential status of the individual.

In essence it probably meant that up to ten million immigrants were contributing funds to the social security system, but could not benefit from it. Little wonder that middle class Americans felt little cause to campaign against immigration. Admittedly, the tone of the debate in America has shifted towards the more aggressive. As unemployment has risen the prospect of a mass movement of displaced people becomes increasingly possible and terrorism has added new anxiety. Nonetheless, by comparison with Britain, America remains remarkably tolerant towards immigrants.

During his tenure as Secretary of State for Labor, Professor Ray Marshall illustrated this tolerance to me with some figures on the 'apprehension of illegal workers'. He showed me how the Immigration Department's graph for 'apprehensions' always showed a leap in numbers just before Christmas. Marshall explained that the department received many more phone calls in this period warning it of places where illegal (especially Mexican) immigrants were employed. The workers were then caught and shipped back home. That is, they were shipped back home for Christmas. Marshall assumed that in the New Year they would then join the flood of illegal immigrants coming over the border into the United States.

Republicans return

In the run-up to the 1980 presidential election campaign most opinion polls put Jimmy Carter ahead of his Republican opponent Ronald Reagan. Few of my embassy colleagues predicted, in their reports home, that the nation would soon have a Republican administration. I stood out among the few that did so. I knew that the unions had no faith in Carter. Only a year before the election I had listened as the President faced severe criticism from George Meany only hours before the President addressed the same audience.

For all its manifest weaknesses, the American Labour Movement still provides essential machinery within the election process. The Political Education Committees are well organized and crucially important in the development of support for a Democratic presidential candidate.

Apart from the blow to Carter's credibility through the Iran hostage crisis, I knew that the unions had no heart for the campaign. I had observed the lack of zest in campaign headquarters. I had also detected a sombre realism running through a discussion I held with the likeable and urbane Vice President Walter Mondale. My diplomatic colleagues for their part relied too heavily on the polls, but I saw a Democratic campaign without conviction.

At the election, that lack of conviction translated itself into 75 million Americans who did not bother to vote. Carter won only six states and Reagan took 44. The Republicans also won control in the Senate.

A small number of American unions have a tradition of supporting Republican Presidents. In the 1980 election, true to form, the irascible Teddy Gleason put his east coast Longshoremen's union behind the Reagan campaign; so did the Teamsters and so did the unfortunate Air Traffic controllers. Soon after he took office, in November 1981, President Reagan issued a request to all agencies of government to "adopt an open door policy towards organized labor."He recalled his election promise to "seek the advice and counsel of organized labor on public policy issues". He then charged his departments to "give full consideration to organized labor's interests and concerns."

The misguided air traffic controllers' leadership in 1981 had deluded themselves into believing that Ronald Reagan had some sympathy for their dissatisfaction with their working conditions and pay. They found to their cost that on the contrary the President relished the prospect of a battle with a union willing to step outside the law and strike.

The air traffic controllers' leader, Robert Poli, whom I knew well, had believed that he had a friendly line through into the Reagan camp. After winning approval from the Federal Aviation Authority (FAA) for a 6.5% increase in pay, together with another 4.8% awarded to all federal employees, the union members rejected the offer by a 95% margin. Poli then called a strike despite a prohibition against strikes by federal employees. The President himself warned the union against taking action and once the strike began he gave the controllers an ultimatum to return to work or lose their jobs. Few of the strikers responded and the union believed it impossible for the airlines to operate without their members in place to organize the air traffic control system. The Administration then dismissed the control staff who were not back at work.

In October 1981 the Federal Labor Relations Authority rescinded the air traffic controllers union PATCO's right to represent its FAA members, and the courts fined the union 4.5 million dollars. Showing no mercy to individual workers, the President also barred the air traffic controllers from taking any other federal flight control jobs. True, the PATCO leader had not consulted his fellow union leaders before announcing the strike, but its effect was to plunge the rest of the US labour movement into chaos. Most unions responded by banning their officers from flying. In a country so dependent on air travel that decision led to conferences being abandoned, many of their activities being curtailed, and crucial seminars and meetings being cancelled. It led to a switch in conference venue by the Printing and Graphic Union from Hawaii to Detroit. Sadly, as it happened I had been selected by the union President, Ken Brown, as its main guest speaker and we had built a small holiday in Hawaii around that event. Instead I appeared before the union Congress in Detroit and to the loud applause of the delegates I greeted them with *Aloha*.

The President's action against the air traffic controllers was supported in public opinion polls by a large majority and the other unions saw the complete destruction of the PATCO union as a major blow to their legitimacy. Following his action against the traffic controllers President Reagan issued his rather odd November 1981 memorandum, which required all agencies of government when framing their policies to "consider the interests of organized labor".

Remarkably, and thankfully, during the strike there were no major air crashes in the United States. Had there been so, the public mood may well have changed. On one occasion during the strike I had occasion to fly across from Washington to Colorado with the family. The pilot announced that passengers might wish to listen in to air traffic control on the passenger headsets. I foolishly did so, and what I heard was positively frightening. At one point I heard our pilot being told that air traffic control had no time to steer us around a major electrical storm centre. We had any number of conflicting instructions at various points and I came to the firm conclusion that the only motivation of the pilot in offering his passengers this 'entertainment' must have sprung from his support for the strike. At one point I thought that we might be destined to provide the one crash that would change public opinion on the air controllers' strike.

Labour law in two countries

The British government's radical views on the place of unions in British society thrust me into a major piece of work mid-1980. The Employment Department had issued its Green Paper on Trade Union Immunities and officials were busily constructing the labour laws that were to provide the foundation for a succession of other statutes.

I was asked to produce a major paper setting out the effect, rather than the substance, of American labour law. It was an interesting project, which in essence covered most of the areas of concern to the British government. I looked at the prohibition on public sector strikes, strikes within a contract, within public utilities and on railways. The paper also had something to say on the question of secondary boycotts, on the complexities of picketing and on closed shops, or more accurately, union shop arrangements. I also included the arrangements for union elections.

The Department let me know that the work had been 'influential' and had shaped some of the subsequent legislation. It was not for me to argue one way or the other in my report, but I did add a cautionary note in the conclusion to that substantial paper. I pointed out that there was considerable argument in the US as to whether labour law had had any substantial effect on the balance of power between unions and employers. I quoted as example the US public employees hedged in by highly restrictive labour laws which, in many states, have denied public workers the right to organize, and no legal opportunity to bargain. Despite this background, the union AFSCME was then the fastest growing union in the country. I also pointed out that while picketing laws were restrictive, in some industries, unions carefully ignore the law and the employers rarely challenge them. The crucial factor for a British observer is that the unrestricted picketing techniques that were then being employed in some British disputes would never have been allowed by the law enforcement authorities even before the introduction of the National Labor Relations Act.

In the paper, I put forward a contentious view which may be disputable but which I still believe to be sound. I argued that US labour law had had a minimal effect on the growth, size and behaviour of US unions. In fact it was doubtful, I argued, if any part of the statute or any particular decision of the courts had achieved significant effect. I maintained that, rather than the substance of the legislation, it was the 'concept of legitimacy' which federal law as a whole bestowed on unions which gave them their strength. Similarly union growth had occurred during and following Frances Perkins' period in the Labor Department through the Department's sympathetic support, rather than the supportive legislation she introduced.

This is not to argue that US labour law has been totally negative in effect. The concept of exclusive union bargaining has certainly shaped the collective bargaining system and has avoided the post-war British problem of multi-union bargaining at plant level. But even on this question I argued that the concept of exclusivity was significant, because unions were willing to accept it, and because it had been well established in many US workplaces before many unions were organized and able to challenge the single union deal.

The US at the time of my residence there was almost unique in the distinctive political stance of its labour movement. Unions ideologically and even pugnaciously defend the free enterprise system. They accept and understand the role of profit in an enterprise. They traditionally respond to redundancy by demanding a price but accepting its inevitability. American unions have never challenged management prerogatives in the manner of British unions. But despite this absence of ideological conflict at the workplace, American employers do not accept the unions for what they are and are constantly on the offensive against them.

Diplomatic Credentials

To most American employers a well-managed company requires a union free environment.

Leaders great and small

The Labour Counsellor's post in the Embassy offered an interesting opportunity to meet and debate with some legendary American union leaders. It also brought me into contact with some lesser mortals. Some of the union leaders were social revolutionaries around whom major changes in American society had generated. Legendary figures tend to be either old or already dead, so I count it as good fortune to have met A. Philip Randolph at his Ninth Avenue apartment on a previous business trip to New York. He died the year after I arrived to work there. Randolph, the first African-American to lead a union, founded the Brotherhood of Sleeping Car Porters and from that base emerged as a formidable civil rights campaigner. It was his victory in gaining recognition from the Pullman Company in 1937 that gave black American workers a national example of the rights they could win through collective bargaining. He organized the great march on Washington in 1963 which led to watershed legislation in the 1964 Civil Rights Act. Before him no coherent national civil rights movement existed. But his advocacy and leadership led him into direct negotiations with three Presidents while threatening massive marches on Washington and civil disobedience. With President Franklin D Roosevelt he applied pressure that led to the signing of an Executive Order that opened up thousands of defence jobs to black American workers. With both President Roosevelt and then President Truman he focused on segregation in the armed forces. The subsequent Executive Order signed by President Truman in 1948 oddly does not mention segregation but nonetheless banned it in the armed forces.

A friend in the American labour movement arranged the visit and I treasure the memory of that brief but stimulating discussion with Randolph of his life and his continuing ambitions for America's black population. He was in his 80s at that time, protected by his house-keeper Fannie Cornes and though not in good health, full of wisdom and dignity. I have travelled through Union Station in Washington many times since and am always compelled to pause at the fine statue of Randolph that stands in the concourse.

The 1963 Civil Rights March on Washington, at which the Reverend Martin Luther King Jr. made his moving "I have a dream" speech, is established as an historic turning point in American civil rights. Five other leaders of various black organizations came together with King to promote and organize the event. The principal promoter of the March, A. Philip Randolph, chose Bayard Rustin as the main organizer because of his long experience of non-violent campaigning. In his biography of Bayard Rustin, John D'Emillio described him as the "master strategist of social change". All the strategies and tactics of civil protest that emerged in the 1960's had been initiated by Rustin two generations before. He extended his skills outside the United States, playing a major part in the 1958 Aldermaston march.

Apart from his brilliant mastery of detail in organizing protest events, Rustin stamped the movement with the non-violent philosophy of Mahatma Gandhi. Rustin was a brilliant debater and gifted organizer, openly homosexual, a socialist and a pacifist. Those latter three characteristics did not endear him to many in the American labor and civil rights movements and Randolph had to engage in considerable persuasion to secure Rustin in the central organizing role. I spent time on a number of occasions with Bayard and gained a valuable insight into the way the 1963 March was promoted and managed. He proved to be masterful at the enormous task. The efficient smoothness of the event drew together 500,000 individuals and families from all parts of America, and its peaceful and cheerful atmosphere owed something to the nature of its organizer. Of those Big Six, as they became known, I am privileged to have met and talked with Randolph, and with Congressman John Lewis, who was only twenty-three at the time, and is happily still with us as I write.

When in 2015 I saw the film *Selma* I recognized with some surprise how many of the civil right leaders I had met and talked to in one or other of the five years I spent in the Diplomatic Service. Bayard Rustin impressed and challenged many of my preconceptions about the civil rights movement; John Lewis was less open and forthcoming but nonetheless an impressive figure; A. Philip Randolph was a man of great stature and talent and carried himself with great dignity; Victor Reuther was a white face among the group alongside his brother Walter, and carried his autoworkers' union into the civil rights engagement despite the reluctance of the AFL-CIO. Martin Luther King had been assassinated before I arrived in Washington but I had an interesting encounter with his widow Coretta Scott King at Dulles airport. Being privileged to fly first class at that time I went to the first class lounge. For a first class waiting room it was quite small at that time and most of the seats were arranged around the walls. The seats were mostly full of waiting passengers, but standing in the centre of the room and lit by the central lights, as though she might be on stage, stood Coretta Scott King clutching an enormous bunch of flowers. The whole waiting room seemed to be in silent awe and looking at her as though they were memorizing the glorious picture of this historic figure. I suppose that now with new technology they would all leap into action and request a solitary portrait on their iPhones. I could not let the opportunity slip away and walked to the centre to talk, risking a rebuff of course. She was gracious and delightful and we talked for nearly 20 minutes. As the attendants called out our flight I asked if she always received a bouquet of flowers, which she affirmed was the case and expressed her difficulty in taking the flowers on board. A young attendant opening the door to the tunnel was clearly star-struck and I suggested to Coretta that she might present the flowers to the young woman. She seemed to think that this would be a great idea, but thrust the flowers at me and said she would be delighted if I presented them to the woman. She was clearly a lady who expected service from everyone around her. I did as requested and a young black attendant looked likely to faint when I presented Coretta Scott Kings flowers to her. As we went on board I received a pleasing smile and wave from Coretta Scott King. Not much of an event but still a treasured memory.

Of all the black civil rights leaders I found Jesse Jackson to be the least appealing. We met for a short meeting in 1982 and he was clearly a frustrated politician at that time. He had a mind to run for the presidency and he did fulfill that plan in 1984. Back in 1982 he lacked a platform and was in any case in conflict with a range of other black leaders. Jackson found his platform in 1983 when he went to Syria and secured the release of pilot Robert Goodman, whose navy mission to bomb Syrian positions in the Lebanon had ended when his plane was shot down.

When we met Jackson's responses were negative on all fronts. He commented critically about most of his black colleagues and others in the Democratic Party. He was particularly dismissive of British social attitudes, particularly in relation to black immigration. I did not warm to him and met him again just before I left Washington, but by then he was strongly campaigning to obtain an endorsement for his presidential campaign.

I had long debates with Harry Bridges, the International longshoremen's leader who organized the West Coast dockworkers. Harry had just retired when I met him, having built his union into a major bargaining organization. He had achieved that strength against a history of niggling opposition from the AFL–CIO, which had expelled the union from the federation, essentially as a punishment for Harry's left-wing politics. In truth Harry loved to make outrageously radical statements. To some extent he had an old-fashioned romantic's myopic view of the Soviet Union, though he had no time for cold war politics and was never a political conspirator. Judge a man by his friends they say, and Harry always had employers, academics, wealthy businessmen and media people as his close friends. In subsequent meetings with West Coast port employers I liked to test them on Harry Bridges' credibility, and never failed to receive their endorsement on his honesty and straight dealing. By American standards that union had a remarkably clean record: the 'Mob' played no part in its administration. Harry believed he had a mission and corruption would destroy his objective.

By contrast, the longshoremen's union on the East Coast had a long history of corruption and a rogues' gallery of its officials have served time in prison. Yet by contrast that union's credentials were never challenged by the AFL–CIO leadership. I had little time for its leader Teddy Gleason, whom I found to be a tiresome conspirator whose main qualification seems to have been his talent for staying in office beyond his natural lifespan.

Gleason had nurtured a talented, good looking and personable candidate for the future succession to the union leadership in the shape of Anthony Scotto from New York. Scotto, Vice-President of the International Longshore men's union, had been considered as a possible Labor Secretary in the Carter administration. I met him in his New York local where he had established an impressive welfare and health insurance system for dockyard employees and their families. He was smart and well educated. I recall enquiring how many longshoremen there were in New York and he told me some 20,000 were on the register, of whom 10,000 were in work. "What decides who works and who does not?" I asked. He tapped his chest.

Scotto went to jail in 1979 for corruption. His conviction illustrated the manner of his union's wealth creation. The port employers claimed that for years they had been 'persuaded' to make payment of thousands of dollars into the union's 'social security' accounts. At the trial the prosecution maintained that Scotto held the rank of *capo* in the Gambino branch of the New York Mafia. The guest list for his wedding certainly gave that impression. He married Marion Anastasia, the niece of Albert Anastasia the reputed Chief Executioner of Murder Incorporated, the enforcement arm of the Mafia. Scotto maintained his innocence throughout and served only a short time in prison. Some have claimed that his downfall resulted from Mafia over-ambition in allowing him to be considered a candidate for the Labor Secretary post; a process that entailed close FBI surveillance. On his release from prison, Scotto and his wife went on to establish Fresco, a popular restaurant in New York City.

It would be wrong to give the impression that corruption and New York labour unions were one and the same thing. In contrast to Scotto I like to think of New York unions being typified by the talented and tough New Yorker Victor Gottbaum, who led the union of New York government workers, the AFSCME. He could stop the working of that great city if he chose; though that was not his style. He was unquestionably a power broker and aspirants for political office knew where to call for endorsement. I believe he retired a somewhat disappointed man, his aspiration to lead the national union thwarted by the socialist Jerry Wurf, who knew every trick in the book when it came to political game-playing in the union. Wurf sat on the AFL–CIO Executive Council and took on the traditional critical role regarding Meany's stewardship of the AFL–CIO – a role previously played by Walter Reuther and in a small way by A. Phillip Randolph.

Like many non-conformist leaders before him, Randolph found life on the AFL–CIO Council to be somewhat unrewarding under Meany's stewardship. It is well known that at one major convention Meany yelled at Randolph: "Who the hell appointed you as guardian of all the Negroes in America?" Typically, under Meany's connivance the AFL–CIO did not back the August 1963 civil rights march, though to their credit many constituent unions ignored Meany's attitude and joined the historic march. In his comments to me, Randolph, a gracious man, gave Meany the benefit of the doubt, arguing that it was more in Meany's style to promote civil rights legislation by arguing the case directly with President Kennedy.

I wondered about that theory when I met Cesar Chavez the founder and leader of the United Farm Workers Union. In essence these organizations that Randolph and Chavez had put together were as much civil rights movements as they were collective bargaining organizations. They might have organized themselves to promote improvements in wages and conditions of work but they had broader objectives, being concerned to promote civil dignity for blacks and Mexican immigrant workers.

By the time I met Chavez he had been embraced by the AFL–CIO orthodoxy, but he knew where his true friends were – those who came to his assistance when he had employers and state officials against him. He told me of Walter Reuther's personal

Diplomatic Credentials | 91

support at a crucial time in the formation of the union. By contrast Meany held Chavez at arm's length for many years. Meany, a New York plumber, probably saw the AFL–CIO as a corporate political machine to influence Congress and the White House. Unions were about wages – they were there to improve holidays and reduce hours of work. In order to achieve their primary objectives the unions needed to establish credibility within the political inner circle in Washington. They needed to place themselves in the mainstream of the American political system. Agitation to improve conditions for immigrant Mexicans, or a civil rights battle to open the job market to a black underclass, came uncomfortably close to the left-wing politics that Meany so fervently disliked. In any case, on a civil rights march one could rub shoulders with all kinds of unlikely bedfellows. It was never my view of him but I was left with these thoughts about George Meany following my talks with Randolph and Chavez.

The death of Walter Reuther in a plane crash in 1970 robbed the American unions one of their most talented and inspirational leaders. I had a friendly relationship with his brother Victor who gave me the benefit of his long association with Walter in the turbulent history of the United Auto- Workers Union (UAW). The UAW had a violent history, and not only in picket line and strike confrontations; both Walter and Victor had attempts made on their lives, and in Walter's case the attempt almost succeeded.

Walter Reuther brought his union and its federation, the CIO, into alliance with the AFL in 1955. He led the UAW out of the AFL– CIO in 1968 on a complex set of issues associated with the AFL's international activities. Polarized views on the Vietnam War also played a part.

When the AFL–CIO walked out of the International Confederation of Free Trade Unions, its withdrawal took with it that part of the ICFTU which operated in South America, the Organizacion Regional Interamericana de Trabajadores (ORIT). The AFL then established three regional institutes to promote democratic trade unionism in South American, in Africa and in the Far East.

Reuther and his liberal colleagues in the UAW were far from happy with the activities of these three institutes. In particular they were suspicious of the role played by two AFL–CIO International officers, Jay Lovestone and Irving Brown. Lovestone had been Secretary General of the US Communist Party from 1927–1929 but underwent a total conversion following his expulsion from the party. From that time he worked to promote the American unions as an international democratic force pitted against communist infiltration. As his close associate, Irving Brown followed Lovestone as International Secretary of AFL–CIO. Reuther and his brother Walter accused the AFL–CIO of allowing CIA money to be used to establish the institutes and to promote their activities. The Institutes have always taken a robustly anti-communist line. They seek to strengthen democratic unions and to promote unions that fit into a free enterprise system. In the case of the South American Institute (AIFLD), it is the degree to which it has trimmed its political judgement to fit into some brutal and democratic regimes around which the main criticism of its activity has centred.

While Walter Reuther had initially supported the establishment of the AIFLD, he subsequently opposed the organization when he recognized that private sector corporations would be contributing to its finances and would take leading positions on its Board. Reuther also reacted to the prospect of State Department financial support. Since their creation in 1945, the three Institutes have been largely dependent upon a regular grant from the State Department, but have also received grants from major business corporations. The AIFLD board chairman at its inception was J.P. Grace, the petroleum shipping mogul. I talked to both Lovestone and Brown on a number of occasions and asked if, as trade union officials, they ever saw the source of funding as a difficulty. They always swept such a suggestion aside. They saw the world in black and white. With the whites they were engaged in a war against the forces of darkness. Of course they denied any involvement of the CIA in any of their activities and dismissed as irrelevant the arguments about corporate financing. This activity of theirs, they maintained, promoted democratic unions in all parts of the world. Yes, they said

Diplomatic Credentials | 93

that process was in the interests of the United States government, but wouldn't one expect the American unions to play their full part in internationally extending the good practice enjoyed by American workers? In their view trade unions were an integral part of any democratic society; therefore the encouragement of democratically organized unions was the best means of promoting democracy in authoritarian societies.

I recall, during my time in Washington, an able and likeable officer of the South American Institute for Free Labor Development AIFLD, Michael Hammer, who flew with a colleague from the Institute to San Salvador. Both Hammer and his colleague Mark Pearlman were tragically shot to death soon after their arrival – in the coffee shop of their hotel. They were in San Salvador to assist landless peasants obtain the titles of land they had been granted under the government's agrarian reform. Rudolphe Viera, a peasant union leader, also died. Michael Hammer was buried in a civil ceremony in Washington, Mark David Pearlman received full military honours at Arlington Cemetery. In fact he may well have qualified for that honour as an ex-military officer, but at the time I thought that in death all pretence had been abandoned.

Brazil nuts

It was the AIFLD which inadvertently landed me in a distinctly creepy situation during a visit to Brazil. In 1982 the Brazilian Employers Federation organized a unique conference in Rio de Janeiro. Its uniqueness lay in the invitation to union officials to play a part in the debates. The conference was seen as part of the liberalizing *abertura* or 'opening' policy of the then authoritarian regime.

The organizers of the conference looked to broaden the perspective of the conference by including international speakers and through the US Labor Department I had an invitation to take part. My Ambassador saw no obstacles to my involvement and went ahead with the necessary protocols, informing London with the request that they let the Embassy in Brazil know of the arrangement.

Following the agreement on my participation the Americans asked if I wished to do anything else during my visit. I had just met, in Washington, the Managing Director of the Volkswagen Plant from Sao Paulo, and he had invited me to see the plant and talk to the managers. I therefore made arrangements to visit Sao Paulo following the conference. I then had a call from the AIFLD to ask if I would visit their school in Sao Paulo, where a union education programme would be running during my visit. I checked with my Ambassador again and agreed to talk to the Brazilian union participants on the Sunday following the conclusion of my conference.

The proposed visit to Volkswagen had a number of attractions. First, I had already spent some time at both the Volkswagen and the Audi factories in Germany. It would have been interesting to compare production processes and to see how management practices had been shaped to suit the distinctive environment in Brazil.

My remit at the conference, alongside other international speakers, was to illustrate the nature of British labour relations and in particular to define the tolerances in our system, the boundaries of that tolerance and the penalties for infringing those boundaries. Like most international conferences it had a rather unworldly style; but at the same time we were given the distinct impression that we were breaking new ground.

On my return to my hotel room I discovered a note from the British Consul, registering some disquiet about the invitation for me to visit the AIFLD School that weekend and concluding with a request for me to phone him. At 3 pm his office told me that he had left for the weekend but would I call the Embassy in Brasilia. A political officer there repeated the disquiet they felt at my prospective visit to speak to local union officials.

I questioned the nature of their concern and whether this wasn't all a little late in the day. He had only just seen my programme, though he acknowledged that details had been provided by the FCO in London many weeks before. After a long and tedious discussion he admitted that the 'disquiet' arose simply from his assumption that my visit "might just conceivably upset the Brazilian authorities'.''He knew nothing of the AIFLD, nor was he aware that it operated with the full knowledge of the authorities. He had neither information on the AIFLD School nor details of its participants. I told him that I had no intention of disturbing any waters. I would simply be repeating what I had already said at the conference. The text of my talk had gone in advance to his Embassy and I enquired what on earth he could find in it to cause such concern. He hadn't seen my lecture.

The blunt truth was clear as day. Somebody in the Embassy thought it wrong to have a fellow diplomat from another embassy working on his or her patch. The political officer hesitated. He had no reasons to give, beyond his disquiet and that didn't seem to amount to much, even in diplomatic language. I hurried him along with the news that I had to leave to catch a plane to Sao Paulo. He asked if I would be willing to wait for him to phone back after checking with colleagues, I agreed.

It took about an hour before the phone rang and he came back with a startling new dimension. "I have talked," he said, "with officers from the Ministry of the Interior. They wish to register their agreement with my disquiet and advise you that *it would not be in your best interests to go to Sao Paulo."*

I was stunned and furious. Here was a British diplomat seeming to threaten a colleague with the Brazilian state security police for daring to engage in discussions on his patch. I left Brazil that night on a direct flight to Washington, against the political officer's urging to stay in Rio, "have a good time," and then fly after the weekend up to Brasilia to see him.

From subsequent correspondence between my Ambassador and London and Brasilia it became clear that nothing but sour grapes lay behind the disquiet. The stirring up of a threat from the Interior Ministry was deeply resented by people in my embassy. Correspondence between us also showed our colleagues in Brasilia to be functionally illiterate on Brazilian labour practices and without much knowledge of people in the system. The most they could do was to indicate some brief contact with two Brasilia-based union leaders.

The Brazilian people had an interesting description for the union bosses of that time. They called them *pelegos*. A *pelego* is a sheepskin blanket that fits on a horse between the rider and the saddle, the horse representing the worker, the rider the political and military establishment[4]

When the politics of Brazil inevitably changed it was not the *pelegos* who moved into political power. The local unions quickly rejected those symbols of a past authoritarian society. Many of the local union leaders, ignored by my embassy colleagues, moved up the structure and across into political powers. The central union activist in Sao Paulo the Interior Ministry Officers feared I might meet, did in fact take part in the programme I had intended to visit. That union activist and ex-lathe operator, Luiz Inácio Lula da Silva, went on to become President of Brazil.

Washington and wider

The Washington Embassy post offered the opportunity for interesting contacts with many American business leaders. Most of them were international corporate figures. For the most part they knew Britain and Western Europe and part of the Far East, as well as their own territory in the US. The global business perspective they brought to discussions provided an insight into the ways in which the US corporate decision- making process actually works. They had an apparently insatiable curiosity for inside knowledge on the British political and economic system, and in consequence I had an endless stream of requests to meet business leaders and to speak to business conferences. I had the duty to project British interests and managed to do so in conferences and sessions in 36 of the contiguous states of the Union.

---

4 Some used a more pejorative term for Brazilian union leaders, preferring to call them Baixeiro, a blanket between the saddle which gets particularly sweaty and smelly.

This work with business leaders allowed me to discern a number of potential opportunities for Britain to attract inward investment and these were fed into the Department of Trade and Industry (DTI) system. I learned from that experience of some strengths and quite a few weaknesses in our approach to inward investment opportunities. I returned to this area of work some years later with that useful experience as a guide.

In the wake of a growing concern in Britain about the increasing social and economic problems of inner cities, the home departments began to demand some analysis of US inner city problems and guidance on the way American authorities were dealing with them. That work took me into some of the worst areas of Chicago, still undeveloped after the riots, into Detroit, with its then frighteningly unpopulated city centre, and of course into New York's Harlem.

In all of these economically and socially depressed areas I met some of the most inspirational of community leaders. For the most part they lived where they worked – in the midst of the social problem. Not for them the commute to a leafy suburb.

In Philadelphia, for example, I had the guidance of a charismatic black leader, the Rev. Leon Sullivan. He sat on the General Motors main board and had acquired an international reputation for his 'Sullivan' employment standards, which he framed for US companies operating in South Africa. His Sullivan Principles were later adapted by Kofi Annan as a Global Compact for the United Nations.

Sullivan's church in Philadelphia hummed with activity every day of the week. The building housed a gymnasium, a crèche, a youth training scheme, activity programmes for the elderly as well as all the usual church activities. He told me of his struggle to persuade black youngsters to stay on in school. He had achieved some success with a range of job compacts as inducements for those who did not drop out. He applied some courage, and achieved success too in his approach to the employment prospects for his trainees, attempting to shift cultural attitudes to open up new job areas. He described the negative views of the black youngsters faced with low grade work, waiting on tables in restaurants, as a total block on their ability to progress up the catering employment industry. As long as black youngsters reject jobs because they regard waiting on tables as service and demeaning, he argued, then they deny themselves the opportunity to be promoted to manager and eventually to own their own place. He had a novel approach to this issue. He believed that, in part, their resistance arose from the fact that few of them had ever been out for a meal or had been served food by a waiter. The kids did not even have that elementary experience to guide them, so as the first step in their training Sullivan took them for a meal, in groups, to a local restaurant where they could observe the catering system from a consumer standpoint. Sullivan established similar training programmes for minority youngsters across many states through his organization. When I met him he had over 30,000 enrolled in programmes. He was a remarkable man!

Diplomatic immunity

Happily my mother remained fit enough to visit Washington twice during our time there. On one occasion she came to a reception at the Embassy for a group of visiting dignitaries. As always on these occasions American guests were invited to meet the visiting Brits. I retain a memory of my mother holding court on one side of the Embassy rotunda, regaling successive American guests with stories in which, I guess, I figured as the source of amusement.

Towards the end of my service in Washington I distinguished my diplomatic career by successfully claiming diplomatic immunity. That fact should not go unrecorded, for it is no mean achievement in diplomatic service on the territory of our partner in the 'Special Relationship'. I believe that I remain the only British diplomat to have been granted that immunity in the US.

During our time in Washington we rented an attractive house along the road which follows the Potomac River upstream to the West of the city. The house owner had some occupation which kept him in the trouble spots of the Middle East. He seemed to spend an uncomfortable amount of time in Beirut at a time when the shells were falling on all parts of that city.

One autumn day, in response to the doorbell, I had a legal document thrust into my hand as I opened the door. It took some time to interpret the document but it eventually became clear that the Internal Revenue Service had a lien on our rental payments, in reaction to a purported underpayment of tax by our landlord. The IRS order required me to pay all future rents to the IRS until the landlord's debt had been discharged. This might sound simple, except that I had a deposit on the house worth thousands of dollars, and the lease gave the landlord the right to retain the deposit in the event of any failure to make payment of rents due to him. Non-payment could also result in a termination of the tenancy, leaving us to find new accommodation with a record of non-payment as a pretty poor recommendation to any prospective landlord.

I phoned the IRS to plead my case, arguing that the IRS case against our landlord, Mr D., was not an issue for me; they should settle the problem directly and leave me, an innocent third party, out of it. I pleaded that it would be quite impossible for me to divert my rent to them as requested.

I had a most sympathetic hearing from the IRS official, who agreed with my characterization of my position as being the innocent victim. What, I asked, would be the consequence of my disobeying the order? He advised against that course of action. "We already have an order out to sequestrate funds from your personal bank account'," he said, "and if you decided to divert your money to other accounts we would simply take possession of your two cars." Sympathy he offered in quantity, but concession was not in his frame of reference. In a subsequent phone call to Beirut I talked to Mr D., but he denied owing the IRS anything and seemed disinclined to take any action to protect me. In desperation I saw the Ambassador, and with one mighty diplomatic leap I was free.

This event with the IRS illustrates a less than lovable side to American society: its litigious nature, which produces a good living for almost a million practising lawyers. Some economists have begun to question whether the malaise afflicting many big American corporations can, in part, be laid at the door of the long and expensive American legal process. Lester Thurrow, the distinguished American economist, subscribes to that view and described to me some events which illustrate his point. In the winter of 1982 a Boeing 747 coming in to land at Boston overran the runway to crash into the water. Two people were killed. A year later the relatives were suing the airline, the airline suing the airport, the airport suing the snow clearing contractor, the contractor suing the construction company which laid down the runway. By a horrific coincidence, two days after the Boston crash, a Boeing 747 arriving into Tokyo landed in the harbour, killing a number of passengers. The day after the crash the President of the Japanese airline, JAL, personally travelled to the house of each Japanese passenger killed, to express his sorrow. One month later the airline had settled all compensation claims with the relatives of victims. I understand that the American litigation went on for almost ten years.

Ambassadors three

I have carefully avoided, in this part of the text, too much detail on the many sensitive and confidential issues I dealt with in my time in Washington. These included the negotiation of a social security agreement with the Americans and some activity to detach the American unions from their allegiance to the IRA. Similarly I break no confidences from discussions with three Ambassadors I served, though in Sir Oliver Wright's case the contact was minimal, since he arrived towards the end of my time there.

I had a good working relationship with the brilliant intellectual Peter Jay and with his successor, that doyen of diplomats Sir Nicholas (Nicko) Henderson. Peter Jay was not altogether popular with either the Foreign Office diplomats nor with the British military top brass in Washington. The diplomats worried over whether his appointment might start a general trend, with the government making political appointments to ambassadorial posts in the American style. The military disliked his capacity to master their brief – in a few cases better than some of them had managed to do for themselves!

Jay established a close relationship with Zbigniew Brzezinski the National Security Council Advisor, and used that relationship to master some of the complexities of East/West relations. From that knowledgeable base he went on to question some of the assumptions underlying the views of the military advisors who gathered around his table at Friday morning meetings. It was not a process which lent itself to success in the internal embassy popularity stakes.

Peter Jay and Jimmy Carter also had a lot in common. They were both conceptual, as opposed to practical thinkers and Carter found Jay to be more open-minded in discussion than he had experienced with professional diplomats.

Ambassadors arrive in Washington for very different reasons. In some cases, like Nicholas Henderson, they are brought out of impending retirement by Prime Ministers to handle specific duties. In some cases they are the choice of Foreign Secretaries and of course, in the traditional way, they come up the diplomatic ladder to reach whatever Ambassadorships are appropriate and available.

I had an interesting evening with my driver Keith at Dulles airport, awaiting the delayed arrival of a Minister. He told me of an event leading to the appointment of Peter Jay as Ambassador. He claimed that one evening during Ambassador's Peter Ramsbotham's period of office the Embassy hosted the Secretary of State, David Owen, to a reception and dinner. According to Keith he received a call from the Ambassador's residence very late that night saying he was needed to take the Secretary of State down town. Keith had already gone home and retired to bed, but according to him he dutifully brought the Embassy car round to the residence as required. David Owen awaited him on the residence steps, instructed him to drive down town to Georgetown and deposit him at a suitable bar. Keith told him that it was more than his job was worth and he couldn't possibly leave the Secretary of State alone at a bar. According to Keith, David Owen then told him to stay with him. So they sat there for two hours with David Owen exploding with anger over an event earlier in the evening and working off his frustration. Keith's story was that David Owen had reached a crucial point in a discussion with senior Americans attending the dinner when, without warning, the Ambassador had abruptly stood up to thank everyone, effectively bringing the event to a close.

According to Keith he then went into the garage the following day and told his colleagues that a new Ambassador would shortly be arriving in Washington. This 'news' was received with derision at the time, but events bore Keith's prediction out when Peter Ramsbotham was announced as the next Governor of Bermuda and, a short time later Peter Jay announced as the incoming Ambassador.

Many political observers at the time took the view that this appointment was made by the then Prime Minister, Jim Callaghan, the father-in-law of Peter Jay. According to Keith this was never the case and the Secretary of State had made up his mind before he left Washington to appoint a very different calibre of Ambassador. I have never checked out with Peter Jay or David Owen the substance of this story and it remains an anecdote, but a very interesting one at that.

Nicholas Henderson came to Washington following Ambassadorial posts in Bonn and Paris. In Paris he had reached the traditional Foreign Office retirement age, at which point he penned his confidential valedictory report. By a mysterious route, but with perfect timing, his report found its way into the pages of *The Economist*, which ensured that its contents caught the eagle eye of the new Prime Minister, Margaret Thatcher. She approved of its sentiments, persuaded Henderson not to retire and had him appointed to the Washington Ambassador's post.

After the Hendersons' arrival, the modern art that had been brought in to the residence by the Jays was crated up and dispatched to London. They were replaced by more traditional paintings which more comfortably filled the panel spaces throughout that grand Lutyens building. Invitations to the Ambassador's lunches and dinners, under the guidance of Lady Henderson, were again keenly sought by top Washington political figures. Under her skillful eye the rose garden again flourished. The change from the young, intellectual and socially ambitious Jays to the more diplomatically sophisticated Hendersons also reflected a sharp change in Washington lifestyle.

I made my first visit to Washington during the Kennedy administration. The District had a bubbly vitality about it then: film stars flocked into town by the hundred; receptions were invariably black tie and dinner jacket, and the social events were usually full of glitz. My next few visits were during the Nixon era. By that time Washington, a political chameleon of a town, had for me an unavoidable air of conspiracy. The change of administration from the Democratic Jimmy Carter to the Republican Ronald Reagan also manifested itself in changes in both the acceptable standards of dress and in the style of official receptions. With Reagan's inauguration the business community returned in force, bringing with it a distinctive social ethos.

As with Presidents, so each British Ambassador sets both the intellectual tone and the dress style for his period in office. Ambassadors, for combined security reasons and confidentiality, tend not to dine out in restaurants. Against this general protocol I nonetheless proposed a lunch at Tiberio's for Henderson and the new AFL–CIO President Lane Kirkland in order to establish a relationship. I knew that they had at least one thing in common – a taste for and expert knowledge of good French wine. At the lunch they jointly thrust the choice of wine on me. The wine waiter, watching my hesitating hand moving slowly down the page, with the price increasing with each move, bent to whisper advice. "*With these two gentlemen you would be better somewhere near the bottom.*" I cannot recall the wine but I do remember the bill; for the modest quantity of wine set my expenses back for the rest of the year.

The meal at Tiberio's concluded with a somewhat uncanny experience. The wine waiter returned to the table when the two guests had departed. He confided that he had served me many times before, but 4,000 miles away in London at the Hostaria Romana restaurant. On a trip back to London I ate there again to be greeted with the news of their ex-colleague, who had written to tell them of the encounter. Sadly that lively eating house, which consistently served the best lamb in London, is now long since closed.

I served in Washington during the Falklands war against Argentina and observed Henderson's tireless and skillful involvement with the White House and State Department during the crisis. I also saw most of the telegram traffic between London and the Embassy during that period, some of the text was frankly hair-raising.

Foreign Office telegrams tend to be drafted in a distinctly cryptic style with a sprinkling (from senior level) of ironic humour. A colleague, David Thomas, achieved promotion from Washington to become Ambassador, in Cuba. Soon after his arrival an armed intruder found his way into the Havana Embassy and into the Ambassador's room, where he held David Thomas at gunpoint. After some considerable time the Ambassador persuaded the man that they could both benefit from a drink, so the gunman allowed David Thomas to ring his assistant with a request for refreshments. Once in the room the assistant managed to overpower the gunman. The resulting telegram from the Foreign Secretary, Lord Carrington (copied to Washington) was a classic of its kind.

AMBASSADOR THOMAS
CONGRATULATIONS ON YOUR
CHOICE OF MANSERVANT
CARRINGTON

In my time in Washington I observed high drama, tragedy and farce. I sat in the union convention on 31st March, 1981 to hear President Reagan, and was there when John Hinckley shot Reagan and James Brady and two other security officers on the rainy pavement outside with a .25 handgun he had picked up in a pawnshop.

Hinckley had an obsession with the actress Jodie Foster, who played the lead female role in the film the Taxi Driver. He had followed Jodie Foster to Yale University where she had gone to continue her studies following the filming and stalked her throughout a long period. He was acting out the part in the film which included the assassination of a President and had been arrested for stalking President Jimmy Carter. He then turned his attention to President Reagan following his election, and by some bizarre means hoped that by assassinating a President he would become acceptable to the actress. Hinckley's attempt to fire his gun at President Reagan had been foiled by security officers, and the President was actually hit by a ricochet bullet rebounding from his car. The President was said to carry that bullet with him wherever he went following his remarkable recovery.

The assassination attempt was a profound shock for everybody in Washington and outside the city. It of course increased security everywhere and restarted the whole debate over gun ownership. Inside the hall during this event we were locked down from leaving the conference and word quickly spread through the hall that the President had been shot. The atmosphere was electric to say the least. Although these were not natural Reagan supporters there was profound anger that anyone should attack the President in this way. When the Ambassador found I had been in the hall he wanted to hear from me, but of course I knew less than I would if I had been standing outside rather than inside the hall.

On 13 January 1982 I happened to be driving in the snow adjacent to the Potomac's 14th Street bridge, when the Boeing 737 Air Florida plane bound for Tampa from National Airport ploughed into the bridge, killing all but five people in the plane and some of those driving cars over the bridge. Not long after this I was present at the glittering occasion of Margaret Thatcher's embassy dinner, with President Ronald Reagan as principal guest. I spent some hours in enraptured discussion with the Democratic Speaker of the House, Thomas P (Tip) O'Neill. Just before our departure from Washington I had the opportunity to meet and talk with a man I had long admired, Justice Thurgood Marshall, the great civil rights lawyer who became the first African-American to be appointed to the Supreme Court. As a member of the Court he wrote some of the finest dissenting opinions, many of them on cases concerning the death penalty, to which he was implacably opposed, and on issues of discrimination.

Before his appointment to the Supreme Court he led many cases but the Brown v Board of Education, Topeka Kansas, judgment by the Court proved to be a landmark decision and his leadership of the case for the NAACP established his reputation. The Court determined that public (State) schools were in breach of constitutional rights where they established separate educational establishments for black and for white students. The Court ruled that "separate educational facilities are inherently unequal." For the Civil Rights movement it was a major success and it paved the way for integration in public school education and beyond. Chief Justice Earl Warren wrote the Opinion and worked to effect a unanimous decision on it by the Court. The Court ruling resulted in some rather wild reactions from a small number of Governors from Southern states and it took considerable time before the achievement of a fully integrated public educational system across the States. I thought it significant that President George W Bush should commemorate the 50th anniversary of the Brown case by celebrating it as "a decision that changed America for the better and forever".

Justice Marshall was fairly abrupt in his responses at first, but warmed when I mentioned that I had met A. Philip Randolph. Marshall told me that his father had worked on the Pullman Cars. He relaxed even more when I told him that I had read his minority dissenting opinion in the Texas San Antonio School District Case in which he had argued that education is a fundamental constitutional right. I managed to get him to talk a little about his early experiences as a civil rights lawyer, often working in hostile environments in the South.

Diplomatic Credentials | 107

As time drew near for our return to Britain, we began to realize how great a wrench that departure would be. We would miss our American friends and the open nature of American society. We would also miss the warmth of the summer days and rattling cicadas. Most of all we would miss Alyce, who had decided to stay in America. However, there were many treasured memories to take with us. Among them was one glorious evening on Independence Day, sitting on the steps of the Capitol building as Aaron Copland below us conducted the National Symphony Orchestra. As the percussion boomed the final chords of his *Fanfare for the Common Man* the fireworks lit the sky, the Mall and the distant Lincoln Memorial in a harmonic blaze of coloured light.

* * * *

Following our departure we returned to the States many times, particularly to visit Alyce and our grandchildren. I also took a job that would enable me to do business in the States. On one occasion in 2001, I returned to speak at the funeral of Stanley Ruttenberg. It struck me, as at similar memorial services, that each of the speakers provided a highly focused glimpse of our friend's life and achievements. Each speaker provides a piece of a jigsaw which gradually produces a rounded view. In the case of my friend Stanley Ruttenberg I contributed my knowledge of him over the final twenty-five years of his life. I knew that he had held a distinguished post as Assistant Secretary of Labor in the Johnson administration, and before that had worked as an economist in the AFL-CIO. I also knew that Stanley had been brought in to the Johnson administration to introduce employment programmes that would eliminate widespread racial discrimination, especially in State government offices. Stanley never spoke of the reasons why Johnson had chosen him to undertake that task. At the funeral ex-senator Gaylord Nelson provided an illuminating glimpse of Stanley's life and motivation. Nelson explained that Stanley and he had both served as lieutenants in the US army in the Okinawa campaign. Both Stanley and he had headed platoons made up of black conscripts, whom the army had judged lacked the qualities needed to lead their own platoons. Stanley had a black second lieutenant below him with a degree from Harvard who was still not judged competent, nor as having the necessary leadership qualities. Stanley ended the war with the highest regard for all the men in his platoon.

After his discharge from the army Stanley returned home with a burning resentment against discrimination in all walks of life. It was this conviction about the need for an equitable society that attracted Johnson to appoint Stanley to his administration. In that position as Assistant Secretary of State for Labor Stanley was responsible for investigating complaints of discrimination throughout the state employment services. The federal government at that time financed the employment services but the individual states managed the agency's local programmes. By threatening and cutting employment services money, Stanley gained the compliance required to remove discriminatory practices and pave the way for the greater employment opportunities that marked the Johnson administration.

Six Home Again

... to trouble...

The instruction to return to Britain came as suddenly as had the original opportunity to go to Washington. A phone call around 6.30 am offered me the top departmental job in Scotland: it was just before Christmas, but I had to be in post by the first week in January.

The process of detaching ourselves from Washington consisted of a frenetic round of goodbye sessions punctuated by bouts of selling as we disposed of our cars, electrical goods and a hoard of 'collectibles' we decided not to ship home. Putting the house back in a state to ensure the return of a few thousand dollars' deposit also concentrated our energies. In between times I completed my valedictory report.

As luck would have it, just as we were about to leave the post in Scotland disappeared under Secretary of State Norman Tebbit's iron heel. We thus arrived at a cold and rainy Heathrow with no job, and a house devastated by its last tenants to which we vowed we would never return. We thus moved in with some generous friends at a college they ran in Ruislip to allow time to reflect on our position and to await developments.

At this point I gave serious thought to leaving the civil service, possibly to return to the States. I had been through some probing meetings with American colleagues in a number of organizations in New York and in Washington. They had raised the question of my staying to take on a job with them. I had no doubt that I could find a stimulating and profitable occupation were I to take the next plane back. But life is never that simple. Steve was still at college completing his MA, and might need help and a base. Both Geraldine and I had elderly parents needing support. Our goods and chattels were in a container heading for Britain. Nonetheless I came very close to buying a return ticket.

Then the Secretary of State's office phoned to say that he wished to see me. There are two Norman Tebbits: the best known one, the populist politician, wrapping himself in the union flag, sneeringly contemptuous of collectivist institutions such as the European Community, trade unions and the welfare state. Then there is the Tebbit one meets in private, employing good-natured banter and jokes, a willingness to debate and to consider ideas. It was this latter Norman Tebbit with whom civil servants of most persuasions enjoyed working.

At our meeting we talked around the work I had done in America. He complimented the style and content of my reports and said that he had enjoyed reading my valedictory paper. He moved on to test out my views on the place of law in labour relations. I referred him to my report of the functioning of American labour law, which from an American perspective covered all the main aspects of the Department's Green Paper. In my view the law had to be balanced in its construction of rights and obligations, making provisions and demands on all sides equally. Labour Law in particular needed to avoid providing lawyers with a lucrative living at the expense of employers and workers. The law also needed to provide open and equal access. To have long-term credibility, I argued, the law had to be acceptable to those to whom it applied. Set against these standards, I told him, the British government's labour law proposals were seriously deficient. He asked for a practical example and I responded that a viable legal framework had to include provisions which allowed unions to achieve recognition rights. At the end of the discussion Tebbit said that he did not agree with many of my basic premises, but that had we engaged in the debate prior to his decision on Scotland then I would have been appointed to the post. It was gracious of him to admit his error in private. But I could not pass up the chance to say that it should be fairly easy for a Secretary of State to arrange events in just that way, should they have a mind to do so.

On the same day as my discussion with Tebbit the Department made me offers of a number of jobs, from among which I chose to go initially to the Manpower Services Commission headquarters in Sheffield, and then to the Northern Regional Director's post. The job had an added responsibility to establish inner city regeneration teams to promote economic activity in the cities of Newcastle, Sunderland, Darlington and Middlesbrough.

An art lesson

It was an oddity of that short-term Sheffield job that a lot of the serious work had to be done in London. Where that required an overnight stay, if alone, I took to eating at Wheelers in Soho. Perched on a stool at the counter I would invariably find someone interesting to talk to over the meal. On one such evening around the end of May 1985, I found myself sitting at the end of the counter next to a gnomish-looking fellow wearing a leather jacket. He gave the impression that he had been drinking for some time and insisted that I join him in sharing his wine. He was similarly persuasive in ordering a joint helping of whitebait which I at first resisted, on the grounds that I could not stomach all those staring eyes. Finally I gave way and we shared an enormous plate together. As we ate and drank, he enquired if I had any experience of printing and design. He had an exhibition recently opened but, in his view, the "incompetent reproduction and shoddy layout of the catalogue", which he claimed had been undertaken by top designers and printers, threw into question the ability of anybody in Britain to produce a catalogue of first class quality. "Do we have to go to Italy to get the quality all major exhibitors expect?", he asked.

Having previously told him of my recent return from America, my companion enquired if I liked any American art. I mentioned a liking for Andrew Wyeth and Edward Hopper. Most of all though, I admitted to enjoying Georgia O'Keefe: her work was so redolent of the desert areas of New Mexico. Her art had grown out of her environment. My companion rejected that notion. There was a good chance, he argued, that O'Keefe had gone to that environment because it suited her art, and her arthritis!

The conversation wandered through various subjects, such as which European city I liked best; did I like Australian wine? (somewhat of a novelty at that time), and what did I think of Spain? But the discussion always kept coming back to aspects of art. My companion asked if I had been to any art exhibitions during my stays in London and we briefly discussed some of the art I had seen in the previous few months. "What motivates a civil servant'?" he enquired. "What motivates an artist'?" I responded. "A typical civil service response'" he quietly rapped back. But he told me what motivated him. For him, it was simply a process of interpreting his senses and translating that interpretation into images.

I slowly recognized my own stupidity. I had been engaged for two hours in a discussion with Francis Bacon. When we parted, he paid me the compliment of saying that, though I knew little about art, I did know a lot about the way to argue a case and we should meet at Wheelers again for a drink. Sadly, soon after, Wheelers chose to 'tart up' their restaurant, losing his custom and mine.

In the thankfully short time I spent at the Manpower Services Commission (MSC) I had the testing experience of dealing with the decidedly oddball Minister of State, Peter Morrison. His reputed capacity for hard drinking and the alarming rumour of him being apprehended by police on suspicion of deviant behaviour had clearly stamped him with the label: "Treat with care." Morrison added to that health warning by his practice of marching around the MSC building at 8am and charging into rooms to see if he could find anyone having an early morning read of *The Guardian*—his *bête noire*. To his delight he once discovered some of my staff playing early morning computer games and castigated them for wasting taxpayer's money. It was a typically stupid act and I had the pleasure of telling him that the 'game' was part of a structured computer-training programme. I had to ask if he didn't think it wise to leave the management of the staff to me and for him to concentrate on policy.

However, the really interesting confrontation with Morrison came later when I met him at his Ministerial office in London. One small bit of work carried out during my Directorate concerned the sponsorship of training programmes for managers in industry. Morrison asked me to run through each programme, giving its objectives and the target management group. I had never thought highly of all the programmes but I did hold the view that, measured by the best international standards, British management at that time had plenty of room for improvement. The programmes were based on the premise that well-designed, accurately targeted and effectively managed training could improve performance. It was a view supported by the main employer federations.

Morrison listened as I went through the general details of each programme. As I concluded each one he said, "Get rid of it." He was unmoved by the fact that contracts existed with the training providers and companies had paid for managers to attend and cancellation would be very costly. After two hours of this he had wiped out half the programmes. We were then interrupted by the arrival of his nephew to accompany him on a lunch appointment. That would clearly finish Morrison off for the rest of the day so I retained some hope for a reprieve.

I went back to my office, pulled out all the background files on the programmes into a literal mountain of paper and began to work systematically through them. My instincts told me that somewhere in that mountain there existed a bit of evidence that would provide a defence against Morrison's butchery of the programmes. The idea that government money should be spent on training everybody except the managers was patently absurd. In restructuring the labour market, the whole labour force needed to be equipped with new skills. I stayed very late into the night hours and had a neat reward for my labours. A letter in the file from Norman Lamont, then Junior Minister of the DTI, argued that the relatively low productivity in the British manufacturing industry could be attributed in part to the poor performance of managers. He maintained that the training agencies had failed to engage effectively in the training of managers and he called on the MSC to support a wide range of programmes.

On the basis of that letter I persuaded David Young, the Chairman, to request a meeting of Junior Ministers from the main economic departments to hear a proposition for a widening programme of management training. He promised to chair the meeting, but on the day he had to dash across to Number 10 to see the Prime Minister, and that left me in the hot seat surrounded by a Ministerial team containing Morrison. I think that another lunch meeting intervened and Morrison left half way through my peroration, while the rest of them gave my proposition their strong backing. Oddly, Morrison never referred to the issue again. His whole approach typified a capricious side to British politics that has, for generations, undermined effective governance.

Morrison held another Ministerial office before going on to serve as Deputy Chairman of the Conservative Party. To Margaret Thatcher's great cost she relied on his faulty intelligence gathering and unhelpful advice during the 1990 putsch that removed her from office.

Leading the City Action Team

It was with considerable relief in October 1984 that I moved into the Northern Regional Director's post of what was then the Department of Employment. The responsibilities covered the traditional range of departmental functions, administration of the Northern Job Centres, Youth and Adult Training Programmes, job-inducing programmes, disabled employment and all the usual peripheral departmental responsibilities. I also took on the duty that had attracted me to the northern post in the first place, namely the leadership of the City Action Team (CAT).

City Action Teams were based upon the perfectly correct assumption that economic departments of state needed, at regional level, to co-ordinate their policies, activities and spending into a single strategy if they were to succeed in contributing to the regeneration of Britain's industrial cities. It was a policy to which the government returned some ten years later when, in 1994, it established the integrated government offices in each region. In truth, however, the government saw the City Action Teams as excellent vehicles for projecting government policy. From the outset, the seeds of a good idea were almost swamped in a tide of glitz and public relations hype. We were launched by Ministers with a barrage of glossy brochures and video presentations, but no extra money. The CATs were received with considerable cynicism. On the day after their launch, April 19th 1985, *The Guardian* encapsulated this cynicism with a cartoon showing three bowler-hatted musicians, 'The CATs Merry Dance Band', greeting an impoverished musician in a derelict street. "The Lady at Number 10 says she hasn't got any money to give you – but perhaps you would like some music lessons."

In my own role I had to overcome another problem. My co-directors, Reay Atkinson and Alistair Balls, could hardly be expected to welcome a newcomer to be their Team Leader. Alistair became a great support and later moved to head the Tyne & Wear Development Corporation, where he applied his immense energy to the transformation of the economic and social environment along the banks of the two rivers. Reay, for his part, remained his energetically challenging self throughout, though he subsequently gracefully volunteered the view that I had turned a piece of government hype into real economic achievement.

I soon decided that the bulk of my department's work, other than the City Action Team, needed the addition of a colleague with different talents from mine. I had the luck to recruit an ambitious and able deputy, Ken Pascoe, who took over the main departmental responsibilities, freeing me to throw myself into City Action Team activity.

We set about tailoring many of the departmental programmes to meet CAT needs. Then, in a meeting with Lord Young, I convinced him that the CAT should operate in the inner cities of

Sunderland (to meet the problems of shipbuilding decline) and Middlesbrough, as well as the Newcastle-Gateshead connurbation. I also persuaded him that the CAT directors should be committed to work together in all areas of the region.

We needed extra money, and during a deliberately organized long car journey on one of his visits, I attempted to convince Lord Young that a small amount of extra money would produce a major effect, given our co-ordinated programmes. We had the projects designed and ready to begin: given the seed capital to promote them we could show results within months. Within a few days I had a reply from Kenneth Clarke, then the DTI Minister, providing the requested resources. A hectic but rewarding period of activity followed.

The mid-80s saw the North East of England in the midst of its worst economic decline. Coal industry closures were accelerating, the steel industry in Consett disappeared and commercial shipbuilding sustained a mortal blow with the decision by the government not to provide work for or subsidize its production. I went with the Industry Minister, Tony Newton, to meet the Save Our Shipyards Committee, at which he made clear the government's intentions. Immediately before that meeting I took him to the Ropery, which had been converted into a high-tech training centre. Some years before its conversion, the Ropery had produced ropes for most of the ships built on the river Wear. Bob Cooper, the owner of the company which ran the centre, told the Minister of archaeological evidence indicating that shipbuilding on the Wear could be traced back almost 1,000 years. Newton had few of the hard-nosed attributes of the Thatcherite politicians of the time and it would be good to believe that his long period in one public office or another owed something to his civilized behavior. He had the sensitivity and intelligence to see the decision to close the shipyards in its historical context. In effect, it was the end of a thousand years of shipbuilding on the River Wear.

Unemployment had risen in the North East to a high of 18%, but it was also heavily concentrated in areas where few new employment opportunities existed. There were particular housing

Home Again | 117

estates where virtually every household relied upon some form of state welfare benefit.

Yet even in the midst of this depression there were significant signs of the economic investment, coupled with brash optimism, that gradually but positively regenerated the region's economy over the following ten years. John Hall began the construction of Europe's biggest indoor shopping mall. Before shipbuilding had finally gone from the Wear, Sunderland had been chosen as the site for Nissan's European production plant. On the back of that success, all the North East local authorities, together with the business community and trade unions, assisted by government departments in the region, came together to form the Northern Development Company (NDC) as the instrument to continue the process of attracting inward investment.

Not that these developments were received with universal acclaim. Plenty of voices were raised against the import of Japanese 'screwdriver' jobs. John Hall's Metro Centre would destroy the commercial centre of Newcastle. Either it would fail because of low earnings in the North East, or it would fail to attract customers as a result of the low level of car ownership. These views were soon to be proved wrong by events.

At that time negative attitudes were widely prevalent in the North East. One particular academic in the region continued for almost ten years to propound the thesis that inward investment did not increase the number of jobs in the economy and had a neutral, if not negative effect on economic growth. As the long-term impact of inward investment on the North East's economy began to be apparent to even the most cynical of observers, he shifted out of both his university and his thesis.

We determined in the City Action Team to work within the areas of most acute deprivation. We aimed to promote job opportunities linked to training programmes, to provide facilities which encouraged small business, and by concentrating the resources of the three departments, to endeavour to achieve the greatest economic effect by attracting investment. To drive the

CAT work, I took on a team of people with Vince Robinson as their head and I drove them at a furious pace. In four years we successfully promoted hundreds of projects. None were too small and none too big. I still believe that we had a discernible impact on the attitude of business, on the policies of local authorities and certainly on the policies and behaviour of government departments.

Assisted by Newcastle Breweries, we started our work with the conversion of the brewery's old stables: a fine building in a street of Georgian houses which we turned into managed workshops for small businesses needing a city centre location. It was officially opened by Prince Charles.

We commissioned the construction of a riverboat in an endeavour to open the Tyne to tourist traffic. We sponsored exhibitions, developed many other managed workshops and established a pattern of high-quality training programmes linked into job compacts with local employers. We achieved one of our most satisfying projects in the conversion and development of an old, semi-derelict clothing factory belonging to Hepworth's. Ralph Halpern, then Chairman of the Burton Group, donated the factory to the project and McAlpines agreed to manage the redevelopment of the factory on our behalf. In that way, we constructed the Design Works, a centre which eventually went on to house companies involved in every aspect of design.

My career path crossed Margaret Thatcher's political trajectory at numerous points in my various roles. I cannot say it was ever a great pleasure – more a high-risk encounter. On one occasion, for example, I had to greet her outside the Gosforth Park Hotel for a 7am breakfast meeting. I told her who we had arranged to meet her and then said something about the early start for the day. She asked what time I rose. All the way in to the hotel she lectured me on the virtues of early rising and the benefit of adding an extra hour to the day.

A number of us with a line into the political system suggested that the Prime Minister 'might care to consider' a promotional event to sell the North East to the broader business community.

Margaret Thatcher liked the idea and generously agreed to use Number 10 for the event. On the evening of June 6th 1988 a galaxy of big players in British industry gathered in Downing Street, together with the industrial leaders and development agency players from the North East. The PM led the event with a call for British industry to play a part in the regeneration of the North. She implied the role to be almost a moral duty, but a duty that would directly benefit shareholders as the economy improved.

The reception in the Pillared Drawing Room following the presentations provided a fascinating insight into her behaviour 'at home'. She assiduously moved from group to group, pressing her case for economic action. At one point she saw that glasses in the hands of our group were empty so she nipped across the room in order to steer a drinks lady toward us. When one senior industrialist accidentally spilled his red wine she grabbed a cloth and dropped it onto the carpet to absorb the wine. At 7.45 pm a loud banging quietened the conversation. We realized that the noise was coming from an ashtray held in the hand of the PM. "Those of you dining at the Lords with Jack Dormand should leave, as they finish serving at 8 pm", she called. "And take care not to drive if you have taken any alcohol". We had been dismissed.

In my period as CAT Leader we promoted over 800 regeneration projects. So successful were we, in fact, that at the end of each financial year we had a plethora of worthy projects ready to run and were able to soak up the large amounts of money from most of the other City Action Teams around the country that invariably failed to spend their allocations.

We cannot claim to have changed the world with our hectic activity in the CAT. On the other hand, we did generate a lot of jobs, promote a wide range of new opportunities and put in place some helpful permanent facilities. More than all that, we demonstrated the benefits of inter-departmental co-ordination and the best way in which central and local government could work together to promote economic regeneration.

By 1988 the economic tide of the North East had begun to turn, and real growth showed signs of stimulating new business. Tower cranes appeared in Newcastle and the other cities as developers regained confidence. We had an interesting experience in March of that year with a programme organized for Margaret Thatcher. She agreed to deliver the main address to the North East Businessman of the Year Awards and my colleague, Alastair Balls, organized an event at the foundation laying of the new Copthorn Hotel.

A couple of weeks before the visit we received a request to produce a first draft for her speech to the award dinner. One member of our team had considerable Westminster experience and a reputation for fine craftsmanship in speech writing. We had a session to decide the main themes and we welded together the ideas we knew the local business community would applaud, with some themes drawn from central policies of the government. Our speech writer burned the midnight oil to produce a superb address which, in the reading, we could almost hear the inflections of the Thatcher voice. It went to Number 10 and won praise.

At the award dinner, as the PM arose, I had before me the draft speech to compare her address with the text. She wandered through some old themes and then delivered another misguided homily to the business community, which they clearly resented. It was as though our speech had never existed.

The following day we gathered at the foundations of the Newcastle Copthorn Hotel to witness the sinking of a time capsule. The hotel stands on the north bank of the river, overlooked by a bridge, high banks and a clear view from across the Tyne. Armed police were at every vulnerable point. I caught up with our speech writer and commiserated on the waste of his effort. He dismissed the issue with the remark that in the 'long run' it made no difference. When I pressed the issue, he pointed to the time capsule as it descended into the void and whispered, "It's my speech they will find four hundred years from now." Thus is history written.

Inevitably, and quite properly, central government subsequently looked to move the focus of its activity to the substantial task of redeveloping the old and derelict industrial areas through the creation of the industrial development corporations. With that shift in focus, the buzz would go out of the City Action Team and I therefore decided to retire from the civil service. At that point I had notice of the award of a CBE. My immediate response was to quote Jack Benny: "I really don't deserve this – but I have arthritis and I don't deserve that either."

Seven THE FIRING LINE

A move to the National Health Service

As I prepared to depart from my job as Regional Director in the now-defunct Department of Employment, I received a call from Sir Bernard Tomlinson, the Regional Health Authority chairman. He told me of his decision to retire and said that my name had been put forward as a possible candidate to replace him. He had started his search at an early date, not intending to leave for some months.

I subsequently learned that my candidature had been favourably received by the Secretary of State for Health at that time, my old boss Kenneth Clarke, but it would need approval from the Prime Minister. In the event, my appointment to the chairmanship was approved by Number 10 in July 1990, almost one year from the original meeting with Tomlinson.

I never had any illusions or romantic notions about the effectiveness of the old-style, unreformed National Health Service. It was full of dedicated people, but it was under resourced, under-capitalized and unresponsive to modern management systems. It was a service that had led to the demise of father with his heart fibrillation problems when a pacemaker could have given him many years of reasonably active life. Its treatment of my mother in her old age was little better. Years later, when Geraldine suffered repeated heart blocks, the three doctors treating her stubbornly refused to accept the evidence before their eyes and came near to killing her by neglect. The service has always been chronically short of money and the patriarchal dominance of some senior consultants had made effective management of scarce resources an almost impossible task.

Added to all that, the Byzantine administrative structures offered every excuse for avoiding decisions until the crisis provided copy for the press and then promoted some reactive action. The Northern region of the NHS had 28,000 employees within the system, 14 District Health Authorities and nine Family Health Service Authorities. Below regional level, it was difficult to find any ownership of problems as they arose. At hospital unit level, it was a general practice to blame all difficulties on the way the Regional Health Authority distributed its resources. If a major resource problem arose in a hospital and the local press highlighted the problem, then the District General Manager would descend on the unit; take charge and attempt to manage the problem. If the national press picked up the issue, then the General Manager of the Regional Health Authority (RHA) in turn would move in and take charge. Consequently, the system reinforced this lack of ownership of problems right down the line.

Under the 14 oligarchic Regional Authorities, the National Health Service relied on effective management of its resources being discharged at the RHA level. The hospitals and District Authorities resented the authority of the RHAs but were, for the most part, ill-equipped to exercise effective control themselves. Many of them were too committed to the practice of conspiratorially extracting extra resources for themselves by ensuring that their monies ran out for the most vulnerable and newsworthy of patients at a set time each year. Where the RHAs had benefited from good management and sound strategic leadership the system worked reasonably well. Where the RHAs lacked effective control, however, the system resulted in dereliction of responsibilities, a massive waste of resources, widespread misuse of rules to the benefit of some less than scrupulous senior managers, and an overmanning of the RHA structures to an extraordinary degree. One RHA had almost 2,000 staff with 50 in its legal department alone.

When well managed, the RHAs were capable of introducing considerable innovation. Their demise, largely by their own hand, may have removed some capability in the service to respond to the ever-increasing and constantly changing demands being made on it. In the place of the RHAs the Conservative government imposed a civil service bureaucracy.

Despite all these weaknesses, the government nonetheless still relied on the RHAs to implement the NHS reforms. It was from the RHAs, for example, that the statutory and practical processes in devolving Trust status to all the units was driven. It was the RHAs that effectively merged the District Health Authorities and then consolidated their managements with the Family Health Service Authorities. It was the RHAs that were used to inject financial discipline into the system. Without that powerful regional instrument, and the degree of autonomy that came with it, no government could have driven through the major changes in the National Health Service within those four short years.

A contractual quirk

I took on the RHA Chairman's responsibilities in August, but for the most of that month we were away on holiday. Effectively then, my involvement began in September, with a fairly large number of responsibilities passed on from the previous Chairman. Among these were a number of contracts in their final state, but awaiting the Chairman's signature. One of the contracts formed an agreement with a firm of architects, Fletcher Joseph, under which that company would take over both the work and the staff employed in the RHA's Architecture Department. The substance of the contract had been debated and approved by the RHA before my time on the Board. It promised that the company, Fletcher Joseph, would receive from the RHA some three years' worth of work in order to secure that period of employment for the employees transferred to it. The agreement had taken over a year to complete and had gone through numerous RHA discussions and legal scrutiny. It seemed to me that at that final stage it would be disruptive for an incoming Chairman to repeat the debate on the principles underlying the agreement. I therefore confined my questions to those concerned with protocol. I enquired if the agreement had gone through all the necessary procedures in the RHA. I asked if the Department of Health had been informed and whether the contract complied with the policy direction of the Department of Health. I finally asked if the RHA lawyers had approved the detail of the contract. The Chief Executive and the other directors assured me that the answers to all these questions were affirmative. I recall particularly questioning an oddly worded clause at the end of the contract, but was assured that it was fairly standard practice.

So, in my first effective week as the Chairman, I signed that contract with Fletcher Joseph. The employees and the work then transferred to the company and for almost three years the work proceeded satisfactorily, except that the RHA role in capital allocation during that time began to diminish as the newly-established Trusts steadily took over responsibility for their own capital development. Over three and a half years later, I gave a buffet reception for all RHA staff to say goodbye as I departed from the Chairmanship. On that very day, a writ was delivered on behalf of Fletcher Joseph against the RHA. The writ also cited me as a party, claiming my personal liability in the case of that oddly worded clause.

The District Auditor had declared the Fletcher Joseph contract *ultra vires*, i.e. beyond the legal authority of the RHA, on the grounds that it should not have guaranteed any work to the company, but simply have dealt with Fletcher Joseph where that company could win contracts by competitive tender. It was a confused and inconsistent finding with some odd reasoning, but it had the effect of stopping payment to Fletcher Joseph, even for the work they had completed satisfactorily. Thus, in July 1994 we returned from holiday in Italy to find that a High Court summary judgment for damages had been obtained against me personally by the legal firm acting for Fletcher Joseph, and furthermore obtained without notice to me or to our legal representatives.

Getting my own back

Some time later, during a break from Health Service responsibilities, I received from a prestigious legal firm an invitation in my capacity as recently appointed Chairman of the Occupational Pensions Board, to be principal speaker at a lavish opening of their smart new city office in London. Amazingly it was the same legal firm that had pursued the oddball personal case against me on behalf of Fletcher Joseph and had obtained the summary judgment in the court. Of course, I was delighted to be invited to the event, knowing that as I began to speak at least one of their lawyers would slowly recognize to his horror that he was suing his own company's principal guest. As I spoke, I saw one man sitting before me look startled as I mentioned, in passing, my interesting time as Chairman of the Northern Regional Health Authority. Red-faced, he shuffled sideways out of my view as I spoke.

The personal case against me of course went nowhere. Fletcher Joseph sacked the legal firm and transferred the case elsewhere. My costs were paid, in part, by Fletcher Joseph and the RHA. The case had a number of crucial lessons, first among which was: take care what you sign as a part-time Chairman. That responsibility rests with the Chief Executive. The Chairman is there to lead policy and strategy.

For the government the case, as with so many others, also brought with it a salutary lesson. If major changes in institutions, processes and functions are initiated by government, then the Audit Service has to be involved in that cultural development and must change at the same pace. Another final lesson for me was: never rely on your predecessor, no matter how eminent, to have done the work: re-do it yourself.

The Deprivation Factor

Despite all this the RHA Chairman's job brought joy as well as pain. I had a brilliant team of people working with me. Our budgets in 1991 were large – over £1.5 billion – covering over 28,000 NHS staff in the region. At that time, the RHAs had a great deal of freedom to initiate health programmes, develop new practice, and commission capital development. When I took on the job a knowledgeable friend of long standing, Jean Robinson from Oxford, who chaired the Patients Association, suggested that I study Professor Peter Townsend's 1986 research paper[5] on inequalities of health and economic deprivation in the North East. Townsend had been commissioned by the RHA to undertake his research, but the results had not been to the taste of Ministers at the time.

Underpinned by that reading of the Townsend work, together with the growing recognition that the NHS as a whole was a largely reactive system, I developed a whole series of concepts and began to work them into applicable projects. In the first place, with the guidance of Liam Donaldson, the young regional health director, I determined to put in place a Strategy for Public Health in the region. I intended the strategy to be aimed at encompassing all the standards set by the Department of Health, but also to target a whole series of regional health problems. We drew in the ideas and support of districts and involved medical staff, and in 1992 we launched our programme. It was not an easy set of options: it aimed at setting firm health priorities and would have entailed some tough choices. In every round of the budget allocations and planning meetings with Districts and FHSA's the strategy would be used as a framework for measures of performance. It was a failure of my persuasive skills that, though the Secretary of State came to launch our strategy, the Department never accepted the process in general.

The rapid introduction of those early Health Service reforms disrupted the organizational structures and removed the traditional security of managers in the system. The 1990s reorganization was the first of a series of attempts by successive governments, over the following 24 years, to reconstruct the NHS to meet the rapidly changing financial and clinical demands being made on it. While I had a great deal of respect for the capabilities of the NHS managers, I did find to my cost that a group of senior managers in

---

[5] *Inequalities in Health in the Northern Region*, published by the Northern Regional Health Authority and Bristol University, 1986.

posts throughout the region were determined to disrupt any attempt to reform their organizational structures. It was the first reorganization any of them had ever faced. They had the confidence of men, for they were all male, who knew that they had an arsenal of dirty tricks to employ against anyone who challenged them.

Just before the 1992 general election I had the dubious pleasure of featuring in the main editorials of the National Health Service Journal in three separate editions. The articles were supported by anonymous phone calls from a small group of staff. Right on the edge of the general election, with Liam Donaldson (by now CEO of the regional authority), I called a badly-timed conference of all senior managers throughout the region to set out the proposals for the structural changes. We gave an assurance that all of them would remain employed, but most would need to accept a different portfolio of work.

By coincidence, I went to see the Secretary of State, William Waldegrave, some three days later on a totally different issue. He told me that a telephone caller to the Daily Express had maintained that I had put in place a process for lifting out managers who supported the government in order to put in place a cadre of Labour Party activists. The truth was that I hadn't a clue about the politics of the people we were employing. I told him what we were doing and Waldegrave telephoned the Express editor, who killed off the story.

The dogged opposition of the managers to the organizational and financial system reforms pointed, among other things, to the need for a wider recruitment of managers. We considered ways in which we might provide opportunities for a much wider range of NHS staff to step across their own specialist occupations into key general management posts. To engineer this ambition we sponsored a Health Service MBA programme at Durham University, which had an open recruitment for nurses, senior medical consultants, ambulance staff and all others in the NHS who had previously faced difficulty in achieving their ambition to move across into general management. With a recruitment of around 50 students each year from the northern region of the NHS, the programme soon began to provide a forceful challenge for every post advertized. It brought into the general management of the service an academically well-qualified staff who had also experienced life as managed members of the NHS.

From the Townsend report I also distilled the idea of a capitation policy, which respected the existence of acute economic and social deprivation in the region. The closure of the North East coalfields (from 150 pits in the 1950s in Durham alone down to none by the 1990s) had left small, isolated and poverty-stricken communities throughout the northern region. Shipyard closures had created a similar pattern of deprivation in the urban areas along the rivers Tyne and Wear. In some communities, patterns of ill health mirrored those of the Third World. Yet, some Ministers continued to put forward the obscene proposition that the conditions in which these people found themselves were as much the fault of the individuals themselves as of the government that had accelerated that industrial decline, or the socio-economic conditions that had trapped them in deprived communities.

No matter how effective, a health service cannot cure economic and social deprivation, but an equitable service should respond effectively to it. I had visited most of these communities as part of my CAT responsibilities and I now revisited most of them to look at the health provision. Before too long I realized that we urgently needed to move resources into these communities in response to the appallingly impoverished conditions. We also needed to co-ordinate with the other task forces that had been established to tackle employment and crime issues.

A talented member of the RHA management staff, Dr Bill Kirkup (an ex-obstetrician), worked over many months to produce a capitation policy with deprivation as a factor, and we ran it by the RHA and the NHS Executive. It did not find favour with Ministers, who came under great pressure from rural, therefore mainly Conservative, MPs to prohibit the introduction. These MPs feared that any deprivation factor would draw resources out of rural areas in order to provide for the urban (therefore Labour) constituencies.

I argued the capitation policy through meetings with two different Secretaries of State. One called it 'ideologically impure'. I treated the remark as a joke and we went on to implement the policy anyway. The deprivation factor translated into comparatively small amounts of money aimed mainly at inner city areas and at the most needy casualties in the system. The rural MPs were unconcerned with need.

Taking advantage

Under the financial arrangements of the time, the London regions of the health service regularly ran into chronic financial difficulty around the end of each calendar year. To alleviate these difficulties, the London regions took to borrowing from other regions. With inevitable delays in construction contracts we had resources in the RHA's capital account which we loaned out to London to good effect. Over a short period we made over £6 million profit, which we put to good use. I had as chief executive a brilliant young medic, Professor Liam Donaldson, whom I had appointed following the sudden departure of his predecessor. Liam later went on to be the government's Chief Medical Officer and many rate him as the best CMO for generations. He has a superb mind, tremendous stores of energy and very good judgment. We worked well together, began to reshape the system and saw real changes in patient care coming through. Liam put forward a convincing case for establishing a number of research chairs in medicine, each dedicated to an aspect of medicine associated with economic and social deprivation and working in hospitals. It was not an easy task to get the proposal through the RHA, but we did so. We offered the University Medical School in Newcastle the finance to establish five such chairs. We specified that though established in the Medical School, the clinical work should be based in one of five nominated hospitals which catered for some of the areas of deprivation.

Within two or so years, we had put in place three major initiatives that would in the long term alter the way the health service in the North responded to the needs of the most vulnerable and disadvantaged. There were other projects we conceived and saw through. Following a short visit to Germany, we offered, for competitive bidding, the finance to establish a modern cataract clinic, run as a day surgery unit. The techniques used allow cataracts to be removed at an early stage in their development, so that after their operations patients are discharged and back home within a few hours. This contrasted with much of the then traditional treatment which often required the cataract to form a certain thickness before its removal – a delay which in some cases condemned the individual to increasing blindness before cataract removal. It was an innovation quite unique at the time.

The task of merging the District Health Authorities entailed enormous personnel problems, and a statutory process which had to go through a laborious consultative procedure. While I had many doubts about aspects of the reforms, I felt then, as I do now, that the functional division between the commissioning of health care and its delivery is crucial. In the old style NHS, the DHA both funded the service and had responsibilities for managing service delivery. As a result these two distinct roles became confused in the process. The confusion led to priorities being debated and decided mainly in an atmosphere of crisis: the glitzy aspects of medicine received the prizes, while less newsworthy issues such as mental health received too little attention. It seemed to me then, as now, that the preservation and growth of a service dedicated to the concept of universal and largely free treatment at the point of need required a more disciplined and responsive system of delivery.

While I supported the separation of purchasing from actual service delivery, I took quite a different view from some of the more extreme ideologues who had accumulated in the Department of Health during the formative stages of the debate on the reforms. In particular I repeatedly challenged the logic underlying their concept of a 'market' in public health. One vital component in any effective market is an element of oversupply. It is oversupply which allows effective choice. But at the same time as these un-worldly apparatchiks were proselytizing the virtues of a market they were also insisting that in order to save money every region should be cutting out what they regarded as 'surplus capacity'. Closures of hospitals thus began in every region, while in the remaining units radical rationalizations were being introduced in clinical provision. All of that rationalization may have made sound financial sense to the Treasury, but it had no relevance to the establishment of an effective market, nor to the effective provision of health care for the patient. In any case, at that time in a wide range of clinical treatments the concept of a market underpinned by choice was a sick joke. How could there be a choice for the mentally ill? Similarly, anyone then suffering a severe heart attack for 30 miles around Newcastle would go to the Freeman Hospital. There could be no market in cancer care either: the institutions were simply not there to offer choice.

The Conservative government, having put through these organizational changes, never did declare where the logic of their reforms would take the service. The State did not need to own hospitals in order to set priorities and standards, nor to exercise control over delivery. The logic of the reforms would argue that, as in Germany, control should be exercised by the purchasing authorities. The logical direction of the reforms was for the Trusts in the end to step out of the state sector altogether into charitable or some other form of independent status. Private hospitals could then also be drawn into the sector. The defining concept of the National Health Service, on the other hand, is the provision of care, freely given, when needed, not the ownership of the bricks and mortar. That concept of a taxation-based universal care needs to be held onto carefully and diligently. In my view it is in no way undermined by moving the ownership of the capital and the employment of the labour out of the direct control of the state. As long as the state governs the provision of the monies used to supply that care, then the state should have the prerogative to dictate the standard and provision of that care. By moving the ownership of hospitals out of the state's control, however, the process would allow private developers and independent charitable trusts to replace state capital with private capital developments that would then attract the provision of care commissioned and paid for by the state. This was the logical conclusion of the Conservative government reforms, although they never had the courage to admit it.

Just before the general election of 1992, the Secretary of State met with us and asked the regional chairmen to do what they could to reduce waiting lists. Extra money would be provided. We moved into the task with a will. Many patients were sent to private hospitals and I took the opportunity to visit some of them. They did not distinguish their treatment from the National Health Service provision. The NHS was paying, which meant that as patients, in their own minds, they had been treated under the National Health Service. It was a message the government failed to absorb.

Secretaries of State

In my nearly four years as Chairman of the Regional Health Authority, I served under various Secretaries of State. The first, Kenneth Clarke, was a man to all the regional chairmen's taste. He was an intellectually sharp, combative and robust politician from the radical centre ground of politics. At the same time, he was also friendly and full of good humour. His successor, the cerebral William Waldegrave, gave the impression of an academic detachment from the consequences of his political actions. He was, in many ways, too politically sensitive for the roughhouse character of British party politics.

Following the 1992 election, the Prime Minister, John Major, sought to redress his original error in leaving women out of his Cabinet by appointing Virginia Bottomley as Health Secretary. She had laboured at the junior post for some years, but few had rated her chances of a Cabinet post. She came to the position with a personal self-assurance belied by her fragile grasp of the issues. With her elegant figure and handsome face she combined a smooth delivery of prepared briefs, absorbed for the occasion, riddled through with numbers and quoted as gospel. None of it convinced, however, and she found little public favour.

At our regular dinners with her at the Stakis St. Ermin's Hotel in London, the regional chairmen were treated to a mixture of her schoolmarmery and coquetry. As one irreverent Junior Minister whispered to me during one evening dinner: "a politician of the dominatrix school" In reality, she had neither the political acumen nor the required physical attributes to become anywhere near proficient at either. Prior to her promotion, Bottomley had drawn on her social work background to specialize in social care as a Junior Minister. She had taken responsibility during the Thatcher government for promoting the Care in the Community programme. As Secretary of State she conveyed, to my mind, an insecurity in practically every other policy area but that one.

The case for moving away from very large institutional care facilities in mental provision was and still is unarguable. Even in the second millennium too many still exist. But if those large institutions are taken out of service then new provisions need to be commissioned well before, in some cases years before, the old institutions are closed. To effect a humane and patient sensitive transfer, a whole range of alternative provisions need to be planned and commissioned. That requires capital funding, planning, co-ordination with local authorities and other agencies. Bottomley promoted Care in the Community as a 'liberal' policy, talking glibly of providing choice for patients. At the same time she constantly talked of the need for bed reductions and cost savings. When it was pointed out to her that choice requires excess capacity, she dismissed the point as an irrelevance.

There is in fact a demonstrable case for treating mental health patients in community-based facilities. Where appropriate they can receive care at home, for example. But in the view of many informed people in the service, the programme virtually abandoned many thousands of people who were suffering from varying degrees of mental illness or personality disorder, as they were discharged from or refused institutional care. Large numbers of them were destined for the streets, with occasional night shelters the most they could expect. A large proportion of them had difficulty coping with the welfare systems, social services or any kind of employment.

An insignificant extra resource went into the social service budgets of local authorities to help them deal with the effects of the discharge of these patients. Practically no new capital developments were put in place to provide alternative assisted care. As a result the social care agencies were swamped by the numbers they needed to help. As her Ministerial car took her through London to the Department, not even Virginia Bottomley could have failed to see the results of her work as shop doorways filled with sleepers.

Ministers decided in 1993 that they would abolish the Regional Health Authorities, a process that would require legislation. Before they had that legislative right, they determined that the 14 regions should be merged into eight nonsensical geographical blocks. In our case it meant a merger with Yorkshire. A close friend with connections in the Yorkshire Conservative Party told me that the party hierarchy would mount a strong internal campaign to get their man into the merged Chairman's job. The North East is not well endowed with Conservative MPs and I had alienated the Cumbrian Conservative MPs with my capitation policy. That left Neville Trotter, then Tynemouth MP, as my only, but nonetheless strongly supportive, Conservative. To his credit, the then chief executive of the Health Service argued strongly in favour of my appointment, but political reality dictated my departure.

On a car journey to the hospital in Middlesbrough with the Secretary of State beside me, the car phone rang and the driver said that it was a call for me from the Permanent Secretary, Graham Hart. He asked for an urgent meeting. I knew immediately that I would not be the Chairman of the merged Authority. I turned to the Secretary of State and said as much to her. "How do you conclude that?" she asked. "Well", I replied, "If it were good news, you would tell me right now on this journey. But bad news is dirty work for others to do." She squirmed and looked distinctly uncomfortable, but said nothing for the remainder of the journey.

Happily she was not to be the last Secretary of State I had the pleasure of serving in the NHS. In fact I went on to work with another eight. In the meantime I went off to spend a short four years heading up the Occupational Pension Board, following which I returned to the health service.

Pensions and other things

As I departed from the Regional Health Authority, Peter Lilley, then Secretary of State for Social Security, sent for me and asked if I would agree to chair the Occupational Pensions Board. I have the feeling that the two Permanent Secretaries, Health and Social Security, must have met in the gents in Richmond House and my name been mentioned. I warned Peter Lilley that I had little experience in the complex field of pension arrangements, but he seemed undeterred. This was the period following the Robert Maxwell debacle and the subsequent Goode Report. It became apparent that the job required strengths in systems management to see through, as Lilley described it, "the seamless transition" to a Pensions Act and a new regulative authority. This offered a totally new challenge in the national supervision of occupational pensions. The task required a reform of the occupational pensions administration. These reforms had to be debated with the Pension Funds and the providers – and concluded with the design of a new Pension Regulator. We achieved all that satisfactorily and I stepped down in the midst of a general election

There were other responsibilities running concurrently for many years. I chaired the County Durham Development Company through ten years of its contribution to the economic development of that County. I chaired a socially-owned waste management company from its small inception through growth to being a major regional organization. Some of my time and energy went into the film and television industries through the Northern Screen Commission, which I set up and chaired until its merger with other media organizations.

Returning to the NHS

The health service drew me back as Chairman no fewer than four times, and as always the health service work was compelling. In that capacity I had the experience of working for a number of talented and determined Secretaries of State, notably Alan Milburn, who drove through major, patient-centred, reforms and underpinned them with an unprecedented increase in resources.

The sheer scale of the 2010 reorganization introduced by Andrew Lansley came as a shock to the whole NHS System. If he had shown any understanding of management theory I would have guessed that he was motivated by Disruptive Theory. As it was, he conveyed no interest in the management of the service. In public speeches he constantly disparaged the managers he needed to deliver the changes in the system. Many of those managers were about to be made redundant by the proposed reorganization, yet they alone could deliver the massive changes he proposed in his White Paper and at the same time keep the service operating at a high level.

The Management Board of which I was regarded as a member came together in May 2010 to meet the new Secretary of State and to hear any initial thoughts he might have on the Service. Lansley described a new world of commissioning, new local organizations operating with minimum central control and the abolition of all regional and sub-regional structures. The largest slice of NHS money would go to GP groups to commission the services. At one point we understood him to be suggesting that the new service would have no need even for a Secretary of State for Health. Most of the individuals on the Management Board at that time were reformers. In common they recognized that the NHS had to change if they were to preserve quality of care and the principle of universal care for all. No opposition existed to drawing GPs more effectively into the commissioning role. We made the point strongly that we could achieve that objective in six months without legislation and at little financial cost.

By spring 2011 Treasury Ministers and Number 10 had finally woken up to a potential disaster looming in the NHS. They called in David Nicholson, the NHS Chief Executive, to test out whether the reorganization could be stopped, or if modifications could be made to ensure stability and efficiency. The question of accountability worried them too, with Nicholson's job scheduled to disappear in the changes. Nicholson was widely admired, an extremely effective general manager, the NHS and government were lucky to have him on hand to hold the service together. He did not support Lansley's changes but the process was moving and the form of the implementations had to be addressed. Nicholson agreed to stay to see through the changes. The risks inherent in Andrew Lansley's reforms were so great that, in common with the Management Board members, politicians at the No 10 meeting were bewildered by the nature of the changes and could envisage the whole system "coming off the rails". Any National Health system that treats one million people every 36 hours has to be reformed carefully and for the most part pragmatically. Following the meeting the Prime Minister ordered a month-long pause in the reform process to allow more views to be gathered, additional processes to be designed, and the Health and Social Care Act 2012 amended where necessary.

Apart from the reforms, the coalition government's good intentions towards the NHS were demonstrated by its pledge to increase the NHS income by 0.1% above inflation for the first four years. In the context of the austerity programme this was seen as a generous settlement, but there were pressures leading to acute financial difficulties for the NHS in common with the health services throughout the developed world. Given the rise in life expectancy, the development of new treatments and new drugs – even with the increased resources – the service looked to be heading for a shortfall of £21 billion by 2014. Given that Andrew Lansley had saddled the service with a £3 billion cost for his reorganization, it was extraordinary that the service achieved this £21 billion saving.

But by 2014, with £21 billion saving behind it, the sustainability of the service would require another £30 billion income. It was clear at this point that standard methods of reducing costs and increasing effectiveness would no longer meet the challenge now facing the NHS.

The increasing cost of healthcare in all societies is a matter of universal concern. Since the 1960s spending on healthcare has risen faster than the Gross Domestic Product in most European

Union states – from just above 3% in the 1960s to 8.8% in 2007. But of course the relationship between the share of GDP spent on health and the effectiveness of the service is not straightforward. Cuba is an interesting example. With a per capita income of $4,000, it spends 6% of its DGP on healthcare, but has universal provision. Life expectancy at birth in Cuba is just over 77 years, despite the cigar smoke. Cuban healthcare provision, against the backdrop of a longstanding medical supplies embargo, has made a significant impact, particularly in the provision of good maternity and child care. Cuban medical care, taken together with Cuba's public health programs, has transformed the health of the population. Despite that success no one here would seriously use the Cuban healthcare system as a model to follow. But it does illustrate the point that a healthcare system can, within constraints, be effective and transforming at most levels of expenditure.

Bringing about change

In the North East region of the NHS we had already established a highly efficient quality assurance and development system that the Department of Health recognized as the best in the country. It had, of course, to deal with a population health profile which in part was as bad as many third world countries. In pursuit of the goal of clinical and financial improvement we linked with the Virginia Mason Medical Centre in Seattle, where they have applied the Toyota production system to the running of the Seattle hospital. This allowed us to introduce Toyota concepts and practices to the NHS, with its methods of continuous improvement, no fault systems and standardization of procedures to the North East Trusts.

We have convincing evidence that present-day health care organizations worldwide are inefficient when measured by the standards applied in other modern services, as well as the manufacturing and engineering industries. In hospitals, the services are generally organized around clinicians, procedures and hospital administration, rather than around the patient. Hospitals tend to define service lines in terms of speciality fields such as orthopaedics and neurology, rather than in terms describing patient value, e.g. no unnecessary waiting, reduced pain and discomfort or rapid return to work. Under the immense financial pressure applying to all healthcare systems, many top-flight innovative hospitals internationally are now thinking through these issues and seeking lessons from outside the health industry.

The total cost of healthcare in all societies should be a matter of universal concern. Since the 1960s spending on healthcare has risen faster than the gross domestic product in practically all European Union member states. It would be a mistake, of course, to relate successful outcomes to an increase in financial input. That a country's health outcomes are not entirely dependent on health expenditure is illustrated by the spending of 15.3% of GDP in the United States. United States expenditure has resulted in high neonatal care with over six neonatologists per 10,000 births. This compares with Australia with 2.6 and the United Kingdom with 0.67, and yet infant mortality figures do not reflect the relative expenditure on the service. There are six infant deaths per 1,000 in the United States and four per 1,000 in the UK.

*Infant mortality rate: 2015

Japan	2
Finland	2
Sweden	2
Norway	2
Germany	3
Australia	3
France	4
UK	4
Canada	4
Cuba	4
USA	6
Brazil	15
South Africa	34
Somalia	85

Source: World Bank
*Number of children dying before one year of age per 1000 live births.

One major pressure on health service budgets arises from the increase in life expectancy in the developed world. That trend is the result of better nutrition, improved relative prosperity reflected in good housing, improving medical care, safer and cleaner industry, a cleaner environment and reduced smoking. It is also true that even where societies are poor, good medical care can have a profound effect on health and longevity.

In all parts of the world there are many hospitals and wider healthcare systems successfully driving through changes to deliver efficient, safe and continuously improving healthcare, while withstanding financial pressure. For eight years in the North East of England we tested out the application of lean quality and safety methods based on the *Toyota Production System* as applied in the *Virginia Mason Medical Center*. The North East of England has a set of characteristics that lend themselves to a distinctive approach. It has an inherited poor health profile, a legacy of its past heavy industry in coal, steel and shipbuilding. The region has experienced repeated periods of high unemployment, but has in turn also developed a strong regional sense and a distinct independence of view. Though spread geographically across a relatively wide area, the region has a comparatively small population of 2.5 million, and communication within the health infrastructure is therefore good. Finally, to the longstanding irritation of central government machinery, North East regional organizations like ironically to claim distance from London to be of particular benefit. The character of the NE NHS healthcare strategy and all the projects that developed from this strategy have been shaped by these distinctive regional characteristics.

The consistently high rating of regional healthcare provision in the North East did not happen by chance. Some of its success arose from the nature of the region and its history, and the ease with which people from different backgrounds are willing to come together to determine and then work toward a common end. This in turn influenced the shape of the Strategic Health Authority and positioned it as a facilitator, a stimulator of a wider perspective and new ideas, a promoter of good practice and an engineer of sound process management, as opposed to a top-down management role. It was an enterprising position, working alongside clinicians and managers, always on a sound evidential base to promote efficiency and quality. The role proved to be uncomfortable for some practitioners, with the inevitable challenges it posed to ingrained cultural behaviour. Nevertheless, the strategy had an impact on patient views. In an independent survey of the North East NHS, over 87% of patients declared a high level of satisfaction with the service. That is always the ultimate measure.

There are numerous academic studies in healthcare management to illustrate the relationship between a lack of process capability and professional resistance to improving standardization of processes. For example Jody Hoffer Gittell at Brandeis University has shown the difficulties that arise in transforming practices across multiple medical disciplines. Some of the resistance arises from a defence of traditional medical practice, and a degree of that defence might be a legitimate protection of good standards. On a wider scale though, resistance to standardized processes inhibits the engagement of frontline staff in the improvement of their service. Most healthcare workers are under great pressure, work long hours, and their tasks and the judgments they have to make become more complex as medical knowledge and practice develops. This is where standardization of work is not just desirable but inevitable if the service is to treat all at the point of need.

Overriding all the cultural professional restraints, technological development has the capacity to drive standardization techniques into service despite professional resistance. Cataract replacement is a prime example of that process. In defining its role the NE SHA began a wide ranging debate both within and outside the service on an appropriate vision for service transformation. The debate led to the design of seven absolute standards. These standards aimed to align all the regional services in a common direction.

The '7 No's'

- No barriers to health and wellbeing
- No avoidable deaths, injury or illness
- No avoidable suffering or pain
- No helplessness
- No unnecessary waiting or delays
- No waste
- No inequality

With this institutional and individual alignment the region had an advantage in meeting national standards and ensuring budgetary compliance. The alignment stimulated a range of programmes at all levels to take the Service along the journey set by the '7 No's'. A relationship with the Virginia Mason Medical Center led to a distinctive transformation programme which promoted standardized techniques together with the Japanese concept of *Kaizen*, or continuous improvement. Inherent within these, a focus on waste reduction, safety and a higher quality flow of patients through the system were central.

Engaging all staff in a continuous improvement process necessarily implies the disturbance of hierarchical structures. Driving quality assurance and safety into all levels of healthcare management and treatment challenges clinical behaviour. The Virginia Mason experience provided the guide to moving into these deeply cultural areas, pointing to the requirement for a compact engaging all of those involved. The compact entailed challenging well-embedded cultures and winning over the key figures at every level. In essence, the compact is a detailed and extended conversation between parties (employer, clinician, leader and all the team) to agree the nature of the deal. It sets out the behavioural objectives and the new standards for ways of working. It aligns people to the vision and to the methods for improvement.

As the '7 No's' imply, the process is about the journey, rather than an absolute end. The process aims to reform the culture and engage everybody in continuous quality improvement. It does not inevitably lead to more work for everybody involved. The experience from Virginia Mason points to an eventual easing of unnecessary and wasteful activity and more group control by frontline staff. The effective application of standardization to healthcare does not imply a reduction of sensitivity to patient needs. On the contrary, it puts the patient at the centre of the process.

Efficiency can rarely be measured in a single dimension, particularly in healthcare. Measures that demonstrably save lives and have a medium-term impact in reducing costs are too often ignored under a mixture of immediate cost pressures and cultural resistance. The failure of so many hospitals to ensure the use of checklists, for example, despite the overwhelming evidence supporting their effectiveness, has to fall within this category. Checklists are not totally new in medicine, and have been saving lives in the airline industry for generations. The evidence for their use is convincing and supported by healthcare organizations around the world, as well as by the World Health Organisation and the UK Royal Colleges. Interestingly, the initiators of checklist procedures have been medical practitioners, not administrators and managers. They recognize that medical practice is becoming increasingly more complex and human error cannot be excluded, even in the case of the most eminent doctors. Dr Peter Pronovost led the first substantial checklist demonstration at Johns Hopkins Hospital. He then responded to an invitation from the Michigan State health authority to apply the technique in state hospitals. Many of these hospitals are in very poor areas, serving a high proportion of uninsured patients and in hospitals facing financial collapse. All the staff were under intense pressure and few, if any, welcomed the introduction of 'bureaucratic paperwork'.

An informed conclusion, drawn from an examination of healthcare systems in many countries, is that the combination of efficiency, quality and safety does not entirely correlate with the level of healthcare expenditure. Clearly there is a point at which social impoverishment restricts healthcare whatever the will to provide it, but there are instances of relatively wealthy societies with dysfunctional health services that have a less than satisfactory impact on the health of their populations. Crucially, any national healthcare system should be universal in cover and have equitable access. But no national system is immune from the increasing demands that face all healthcare systems. To be sustainable, a universal healthcare provision of continuously improving quality has to establish within its provision a set of consensual efficiency drivers. In healthcare, fiscal drivers alone are too narrowly based; they need quality and safety measures built in to achieve publicly acceptable efficiency standards. Healthcare productivity measures, for example, are deficient if they fail to give equal emphasis to quality and safety.

We were convinced that we were making a real impact on the NE healthcare system when the Lansley reorganization began effectively to dismantle the intellectual and financial centre of that NE transformation system. It had taken years to build and gain the confidence of the staff in the region. Real health gains were being made and yet it had no place in the reorganized regime. We were told to take it apart.

* * * * *

Following retirement from my full-time career I went on to serve twenty-six years in senior roles in the National Health Service. It was an immense privilege to do so. In none of the seven roles I held could the work be described as 'steady state'. The service struggled throughout that time to remould itself continuously in order to meet the increasing and constantly shifting needs of a demographically changing population. The roles could become immensely frustrating, but success could be directly seen and its impact measured in the health and wellbeing of people. This is not just a cliché. We saw dramatic changes in cataract surgery, brought in against some stubborn professional opposition; lives were saved through the addition of new heart surgery units; safety in primary care improved, requiring the removal of single-handed practices; stroke treatment changed fundamentally and the organization of paediatric care was reformed. I claim no more than having had a steering hand in these improvements.

In concluding these views on the NHS, there are two principal issues worth emphasizing with historical illustrations. The first concerns the affordability of a healthcare system that covers all of a nation's citizens – a topic for debate in many countries and one that has continued in Britain since the creation of the National Health Service. At its inception, the establishing bill estimated the annual cost of the NHS at £134m. The Service never lived within that budget and in its first year the expenditure reached £275m. By 1951, when the Conservatives returned to form the government, the NHS budget had reached £464m. Winston Churchill, the new Prime Minister, appointed Harry Crookshank as Health Minister, who took the view that the Service was unaffordable. He proposed hotel accommodation charges for hospital stays, payment for drugs and for the use of certain types of hospital equipment. The Treasury also questioned the affordability of a national service and supported the proposal for charging. This all proved too much for the Prime Minister and he replaced Crookshank with Ian Macleod who, throughout its inception, had supported the concept of a national health service and believed that the state had a moral obligation to provide the appropriate funding. Undeterred, the Treasury persisted in propounding its views on affordability. In response, Ian Macleod established the Guillebaud Inquiry, which concluded that far greater resources would be necessary and should be made available to meet the nation's health needs. This bit of history illustrates the point made earlier in this book, that funding a national and equitable healthcare system is principally a matter of political will. That fact is as true today as it was during the Churchill administration. This is not to argue for unlimited budgets, and in this book, as elsewhere, I have argued strongly for the deployment of a range of techniques, management procedures and clinical improvements to raise the level of quality, safety and efficiency. All the health systems in developed countries are under pressure from the increasing longevity of their populations and the rapid expansion of healthcare into areas of previously untreatable disease. The challenge is to design the processes for delivering necessary technical and cultural changes that will enable healthcare systems to meet these constant and constantly changing challenges.

The Boston surgeon Atul Gawande, in a brilliantly argued article in *The New Yorker*, dealt with the escalating cost of the American healthcare system as it extends its provision to the 47 million of the population otherwise uncovered by health insurance. He points out that the Healthcare Bill has no master plan for curbing costs. He also deals with the insular nature of healthcare practice – an insularity that inhibits the extension of good practice from high-performing providers to lower performers in the system.

Gawande likens the present United States healthcare system to the condition of American agriculture in 1900. At that time over 40% of average family income went to pay for food, and farming employed half the American workforce. Gawande describes the way the US Department of Agriculture engaged Seaman Knapp as a reform agent, or as Knapp described it, as an agricultural explorer. Knapp astutely chose just one farmer to volunteer a small portion of land on which the farmer would strictly follow the innovations and methods that Knapp proposed. Knapp's team used the success of that single experiment to move farm by farm across the country, so that by 1930 there were 750,000 demonstration farms, represented in every state. The application of new methods and evidence-based disciplines revolutionized the then highly decentralized agricultural industry. Today food accounts for an average of 8% of the American family income.

Gawande advocates a similar process for the present American healthcare system. His proposal would engage a centrally promoted innovation team, working hospital by hospital, to produce exemplars of good practice that the team would use to revolutionize the delivery of healthcare across the highly decentralized system.

In the North East SHA, this is exactly how we saw our function. The NE Transformation programme grew out of that strategy and formed the context for many projects designed to raise the quality, safety and efficiency of the NE regional healthcare system. I would argue along with Dr Atul Gawande that, within an increasingly decentralized system, the improvement focus has to be on hospital-level procedures. The complex nature of the changes required in raising quality, ensuring safety, and promoting the efficient use of resources requires local engagement. In that respect anything other than a centrally initiated and locally engineered process is unlikely to succeed.

Continuous improvement does not require a continual disruption and redesign of organisation and structure. But I fear that in the case of the NHS the likelihood is that the service will be subject to many future changes in those structures in the search for a sustainable service.

Portrait on cover by Peter Flanagan, the talented Northumbrian Artist

Postscript

A close colleague who claims to know me as a man of strong convictions, after reading the foregoing script, commented on the absence of a clarification of the author's values and beliefs. The central purpose of this account has been to provide a perspective on my involvement in events and activities for the enlightenment of another generation. My colleague argues that a clear understanding of that involvement requires an explanation of its motivating values.

One thing should be clear from any reading of the text. I am neither philosopher nor politician. In writing of these various activities I have felt an empathy with that distinguished lawyer Oliver Wendel Holmes. When similarly challenged he replied that his values had "surely emerged from the corpus of my dissenting judgements". In my case, the values and beliefs should be apparent from the decisions I made in the variety of circumstances I describe in the text.

When I re-read this short autobiographical note, I see what I believe to be a set of fairly consistent beliefs running as a warp and weft throughout the whole account. For example, I have an instinctive distrust of the authority of the state, though it is admittedly ironic that a servant of the state should question the power of the institutions that gave him employment for such a large part of his working life.

Douglas Jay, my ex-Ambassador's father, when in ministerial office, famously said: "The man in Whitehall knows best". Too often, when it comes to the interests of the majority of citizens, the opposite proves to be the case. Practically all the colleagues I have worked with in public service have been dedicated and socially conscious. Most politicians in government have been sensitive to the public interest. The insensitivity arises not from the nature of the individuals, but from the institutional framework that dictates the decisions. The defensive nature of government process produces an authoritarian tendency and in a democratic system the popular, and therefore the majority interests, tend to prevail.

It is the pluralist nature of democratic societies that counteracts the authoritarian nature of the state. Single issue political organizations, robust trade unions and employer organizations, a free and vigorous press, an effectively balanced bicameral legislature, well-organized local government and a politically educated population are vital components of that pluralism. In Britain, these essential components are sadly deficient.

It should be apparent from most of my work activity that I have maintained a concern for the disadvantaged. I sought, in applying employment law, to enable people to overcome their economic disadvantage. I gave support to the process of collective bargaining that could bring a dignity to the working lives of the disadvantaged. In the Regional Health Service I struggled to apply a deprivation factor in the allocation of funding.

Support for collective bargaining rights has never encouraged me to extend any personal support to those union leaders who continue to bring to their roles the class-war rhetoric of the 1930's. My father and mother came out of that generation who fought in the Spanish Civil War. My father had friends who did so. Their sympathies were republican and they intensely disliked the layers of class structure with royalty at the apex. Equally, however, they rejected the arguments of the hard left. Instinctively they were democratic socialists. It was a natural step for me therefore to take to the 'revisionist' concepts of Evan Durbin in his brilliant *Politics of Democratic Socialism*. Tony Crosland took me further down that road with *The Future of Socialism*, in which he argued that the ownership of industry is an irrelevance to socialism and that the ownership issue simply confuses means with ends. That 1956 Crosland argument echoed down the years to 2003 when a New Labour government established the case for private providers in its reform of the last of the nationalized industries – the Health Service. In reality the National Health Service is a concept – the treatment of all, free of charge, at the point of need. Ownership of buildings and the employment of staff are means not necessarily related to the desired end. It is a concept that comfortably fits my Durban/Crosland-nurtured values.

In my early years I attended the Methodist Chapel, then the Church of England with the mid-week activity of the Scouts. Winter Sundays were miserable days for kids in that mining town and in the absence of anything else to do, church attendance at least offered a community. The Unitarians hit on the unprecedented idea of a cinema show following their service. I became an immediate convert.

Though I have unquestionably absorbed a large measure of Judeo-Christian ethics I have failed to develop a sense of the metaphysical. I have never understood why the possession of a much better developed brain than the rest of the animal kingdom should qualify us to be candidates for everlasting life. Nor can I understand how we are expected to believe that our biologically dependent personality could survive. I can understand the need for religious belief, and there have been times when I would have welcomed the ability to hold one, but that was simply grasping for an emotional prop.

This is not to ignore the spiritual dimension to life. There is something more profound than technique in Mozart, more than words in a speech by Martin Luther King, more than the interplay of human emotion in a Shakespeare play. As Beatrice Webb so elegantly expressed it: "A community of the soul with some righteousness felt to be outside itself, persisting aspirations, a faith, hope and devotion to a wholly disinterested purpose." I can sign up to that.

The Last Hurrah

10 DOWNING STREET
LONDON SW1A 2AA

THE PRIME MINISTER

10 May 2016

Dear Peter,

The NHS has benefited greatly from your hard work, dedication and commitment alongside unwavering leadership and drive for continuous improvement.

We are all very proud of our NHS and your role, over the many years, has played an important part in providing some of the best healthcare services in the world. This, alongside your long and distinguished career as a public servant in the UK and abroad, should rightly be celebrated and I congratulate you on everything you have achieved.

I wish you well in your retirement.

Yours,

David

Sir Peter D Carr CBE DL

BIBLIOGRAPHY

acknowledgements and references

The following publications have been either quoted in the forgoing pages, used to verify facts or, as in the case of the CIR reports, they centre on described events. I cannot avoid responsibility for the analysis and conclusions in the listed CIR and ACAS reports.

Bamber, Greg J. and Russell D. Lansbury, eds. *International and Comparative Employment Relations.* Sage, 1998
Branch, Taylor, *Parting of the Waters. America in the King Years.* Simon & Schuster, 1988
Carr, Steve, *Changing Patterns of Work.* WEA pamphlet, 1984
Crosl and, Tony, *The Future of Socialism.* London, 1956
Dunlop, John T., *Industrial Relations Systems.* Holt-Dryden, 1958
Dur bin, Evan, *Politics of Democratic Socialism.* Routledge, 1940
Edsall, Thomas Byrne, and Mary D. Edsall, *Chain Reaction. Race Rights and Taxes on American Politics.* Norton and Norton, 1994
Flanders, Alan, *The Fawley Productivity Agreement,* Faber, 1964
Gawande Atul, *The Checklist Manifesto* Profile Books
Gould, Professor William B., *A Primer of American Labor Law.* MIT Press, 1982
Goulden, Joseph, *Meany.* Atheneum, 1972
Goulden, Joseph C., *Jerry Wurf, Labor's Last Angry Man.* Atheneum, 1982
Henderson, Sir Nicholas, *Mandarin.* Weidenfeld & Nicolson, 1994
Kessler and Bayliss, *Contemporary British Industrial Relations.* Macmillan, 1995

Lewis, Congressman John, with D'Orso, *Walking with the Wind.* Harvest Books, 1999

Meister and Loftis, *A Long Time Coming, Unionising America's Farm Workers.* Macmillan, 1977

Morris, Alden D., *Origins of the Civil Rights Movement.* Free Press, 1986

Reid T.R *The Healing of America* The Penguin Press

Reuther, Victor G., *The Brothers Reuther.* Houghton Mifflin, 1978

Robinson, Derek, *Monetarism and the Labour Market.* Oxford, 1986

Webb, Beatrice, *Our Partnership.* Longman Green, 1948

Wills, Garry, *A Necessary Evil. American Distrust of Government.* Simon Schuster, 1999

Winter, J. M., ed. *R. H. Tawney and the American Labor Movement.* St Martins, 1979 *Commission on Industrial Relations (CIR) Reports.* HMSO International Harvester, 1972 Con Mech, 1973 Associated Octel Co., 1969 *Industrial Relations in the National Newspaper Industry.* ACAS for the Royal Commission on the Press, HMSO, 1974

Worker Participation and Collective Bargaining in Western Europe. CIR, HMSO, 1974

INDEX

Air Florida 106
Air Traffic Controllers 82–83
American Federation of Labor–
   Congress of Industrial
   Organisations (AFL–CIO)
   and civil rights 88, 91
   and Democratic candidates 67
   and dockworkers union 89
   and ICFTU 68, 69, 70, 92
   and ILO 68, 69
   and longshoremen union 89–90
   relations between AFL and CIO
     63, 69, 74, 92
   and TUC 70–73
   see also Meany, George
American Federation of State,
   County and Municipal
   Employees (AFSCME) 84, 91
Anastasia, Albert 90
Anastasia, Marion 90
Arlington Cemetery 94
Associated Octel, CIR Inquiry 42
Atkinson, Reay 116

Bacon, Sir Francis 113
Balls, Alistair 116, 121

Barzani, Masoud 63
Barzani, Mustafa 63
Bayliss, Fred 54
Belgium 10–11, 12
Bevin, Ernest 4, 36, 73
Birch, Reg 43
Blumler, Jay 20–21
Bottomley, Virginia 134–136
Bournville 19–20
Brazil 94–97
Bridges, Harry 89
Brotherhood of Sleeping Car
   Porters 86
Brown, George 30
Brown, Irving 93
Brown, Ken 83
Brussels 12
Brzezinski, Zbigniew 102
Burton Group 119

Care in the Community 135
Carr family 1–31
Carrington, Lord 105
Carter, President Jimmy 81, 102,
   104, 106
Castle, Barbara 35, 41

Chavez, Cesar 91–92
CIA 76, 93
City Action Team (CAT) 115–122
Civil Service Unions 59–60
Clarke, Kenneth 117, 123, 134
Clegg, Professor Hugh 23, 33, 56
Coal Miners 9–10, 52, 130
Cohn Bendit, Daniel 38
Commission on Industrial Relations (CIR) 40–51, 55, 59
Communist Party, USA 93
Confédération Générale du Travail (CGT) 37
ConMech 46–51
Cooper, Bob 117
Copland, Aaron 108
Copthorn Hotel 121
County Durham Development Company 137
Crosland, Tony 151–152

da Silva, President Luiz Inácio 97
D'Emilio, John 87
Design Works 119
District Health Authorities 124, 125, 132
Dock Labour Board 36
Donaldson, Lord John 44, 48
Donaldson, Sir Liam 128, 129, 131
Donovan Report 40–44
Downing Street 120
Durbin, Evan 151
Durham University 129

Essex 32
Essex College 34, 35, 36

Father of author 1–3, 123
Fawley Productivity Agreement 33

Feather, Vic 36
Finland 17–18, 141
Fircroft College 19, 27, 28, 29
Flanders, Alan 23, 33, 40, 41
Fletcher Joseph 125, 126, 127
FMCS (Federal Conciliation and Mediation Service) 59
Folies Bergere 38
Ford Motor Company 43

Gaulist Party 38
Geismar, Alain 38
General Election (1970) 44
Germany 7, 95, 132, 141
Gill, Ken 71
Gleason, Teddy 82, 90
Godson, Joseph 77
Goodman, Geoffrey 77
Gottbaum, Victor 91
Grace, J.P. 93
Grandchildren of author 108
Grandfather of author (Harry Tailby) 5
Grays, Essex 56

Halifax, Lord 63, 74
Halifax town 29, 30, 31, 32
Hall, John 118
Halpern, Ralph 119
Hammer, Mike 94
Hart, Sir Graham 136
Healy, George 36, 44
Heath government 51, 52, 55
Henderson, Sir Nicholas 101, 102, 104, 105
Hinckley, John 105–106
Hoehler, Fred 32
Holmes, Oliver Wendel 150
Holocaust 8

Index | 157

Hostaria Romana 105
Hydrofoil on Thames 57

ICFTU (International Confederation of Free Trade Unions) 68, 69, 70, 73, 92
ILO (International Labour Organization) 55, 68, 69, 73
Immigration, US 80–81
Industrial Relations Act (1971) 46, 49
Internal Revenue Service (IRS) 100
International Club, Washington 69
International Harvester 42, 55
International Union of Socialist Youth 17
Inverness 16

Jackson, Reverend Jesse 89, 106
Jay, Douglas 150
Jay, Peter 24, 101–102, 103
Jenkins, Clive 23, 36, 66
Jones, Jack 36, 51, 59–60

Kennedy, President John F. 25, 26, 91, 104
Kikuyu 24–25
King, Coretta Scot 88
King, Reverend Martin Luther 87, 88
Kirkland, Lane 73, 104
Kirkup, Dr Bill 130
Kissinger, Henry 69

Labor Department, US 94
Labour Counsellor 56, 62, 63, 65, 86
Lansley, Andrew 138, 139
Lee, Ernie 66
Lilley, Peter 137

Longshoremen 82
Lovestone, Jay 93

Major, John 134
Manpower Services Commission 113
Manpower Services Commission (MSC) 112
Marshall, Ray 81
Marshall, Thurgood 107
Marsh, Arthur 32
Maxwell, Robert 137
Mboya, Tom 24, 25–26
McCarthy, Lord 56
Meany, George 25, 26, 55, 66–70, 71, 72–73, 77, 81, 91, 92
Mexican immigrants 81, 91, 92
Mikoyan, Anastaz 71–72
Milburn, Alan 138
Mondale, Vice President Walter 81
Morrison, Peter 113–114, 1154
Mother of author 2, 3, 10, 23, 29, 99, 123
Mountain Rescue, RAF 13–14
Murdoch, Rupert 61
Murray, Len 70–71

National Board for Prices and Incomes (NBPI) 33, 34, 35
National Health Service (NHS) 123–149, 152
  defining concept 133, 152
National Industrial Relations Court (NIRC) 46
National Labor Relations Act US 65, 85
Newcastle Breweries 119
Newcastle upon Tyne 112, 117, 118, 121, 131, 133

158 | It occurred to me

Newton, Tony 117
Nissan 118
Northern Development Company (NDC) 118

Obama, Barak 26
Occupational Pensions 127, 137
O'Neill, Tip 106
Organizacion Regional Interamericana de Trabajadores (ORIT) 92

Padgate, RAF 13
Paris student campaign 37
Pascoe, Ken 116
PATCO US air traffic controllers 83
Pay Board 35, 52, 53, 54, 55
Pay relativities 53
Pearlman, David 94
pelegos (Brazil) 97
Perkins, Francis 85
Poli, Robert 82
Pollak, Harry 76

RAF 13–16
Randolph, A. Philip 86–87, 88, 91, 107, 155
Reagan, President Ronald 68, 82–83, 104, 105–106
Regional Health Authority (RHA)
 abolition of 125, 136
 author as chairman of 123, 125, 127, 134
 and Fletcher Joseph 125–127
 funding research chairs 131
 and NHS management 124–125, 128–129
Reuther, Victor 66, 69–70, 88, 93
Reuther, Walter 55, 69, 70, 71–72, 88, 91–92, 93

Robinson, Derek 33, 35, 52
Robinson, Jean 128
Robinson, Vince 119
Royal Commission on the Press 60
Ruskin College 20–21, 24–26, 27, 28
Rustin, Bayard 87, 88
Ruttenberg, Stanley 108

Sauvageot, Jacques 38
Scotto, Anthony 79, 90
Shah, Eddie 61
Shop Stewards 31–32
Singleton, Norman 41
Sorbonne 37, 38
Sterling Crisis (1966) 34
Sullivan, Reverend Leon 98, 99
Summerskill, Shirley 30
Syndicato Mafiosi 48

Tailby, Harry (author's grandfather) 5
Tawney, Professor R. H. 63–64, 65, 73–74
Tebbit, Norman 110, 111–112
Thatcher, Margaret 103, 106, 115, 119–120, 121
Thomas, David 105
Thurrow, Lester 101
Tiberio's 104
Tokyo 101
Tomlinson, Sir Bernard 123
Trotter, Sir Neville 136
TUC (Trades Union Congress)
 and AFL-CIO 70–73
 and CGT 37
 and collective bargaining 32
 and First Division Association 23

Index | 159

and Industrial Relations Act (1971) 46, 49
and shop stewards 31

Viera, Rudolphe 94
Virginia Mason Medical Centre 140, 142, 144, 145
Volmer, Rudolph 78

Waldegrave, William 129, 134
Washington DC 62–65

Webb, Beatrice (quote) 152
Weiner, Herb 76
Wheelers in Soho 112, 113
Wilberforce Inquiry 52
Woodcock, George 40–41, 44, 45, 51
Wright, Sir Oliver 101
Wurf, Jerry 91

Young, David (Lord) 115, 116, 117